Gillian Hooper joined the NHS as a student nurse in 1977; set 447 at the Princess Alexander School of Nursing – The London Hospital, Whitechapel. Specialising in Cardiothoracic Intensive Care, she worked at the London Chest Hospital prior to become an ITU sister at the now closed Middlesex Hospital. She undertook a master's in Healthcare Management at City University prior to securing her first Executive Director of Nursing/Quality and Community Services position at the Northern Devon Healthcare Trust in 1994. Four years later, she was appointed Director of Nursing and Deputy CEO at West Hertfordshire Hospitals NHS trust, providing general hospital and regional specialist services across four hospital sites. Stimulated by a major NHS reorganisation, she took the opportunity to lead a national team of service improvement managers improving patient access on behalf of the Modernisation Agency, where she developed a forensic knowledge of root-cause-analysis and how to effectively manage capacity and demand. She was invited to design and implement an innovative approach to commissioning acute services on behalf of four Primary Care Trusts (PCTs) serving the population of East and North Hertfordshire and in 2007, she was appointed the national lead for a 2-year commercial partnership programme aiming to build world class commissioning capacity and capability within PCTs. As Director of Quality and Commissioning for the London Deanery, she led investigations into high-risk patient safety concerns across London and led an organisational transition programme to Health Education England, in addition to designing and leading a £325m competitive procurement process establishing lead educational providers of Medical and Dental education across London. She was awarded an NHS London Leadership Award for this work in 2011. It was during this time that Gillian commenced her working with the CQC, as an independent clinical chair, where she chaired 12 comprehensive organisational wide inspections across hospital, community, ambulance and independent sectors. In 2014, Gillian began to establish an independent portfolio of part time appointments: to provide bespoke support to trusts. She was appointed by Monitor as a Turnaround Director to support multiple trusts in special measures, to develop improvement plans and strengthening assurance processes. A strong supporter of the work of the Florence Nightingale Foundation she has mentored leadership scholars, in 2018, she accepted a 2-year appointment as the CQC's National Professional Advisor – Well led Reviews, where she developed assessment frameworks, contributed to numerous inspections, trained inspectors, developed the role of the trust Executive Reviewer and pioneered a risk-based approach to undertaking reviews. In 2019, she was appointed by KPMG as a Clinical Leadership Associate and the following year appointed to an Honorary Readership in the School of Health Sciences for the University of East Anglia. Gillian continues to provide bespoke support to leadership teams in trusts as part of a portfolio of work, whilst her family continues to increase the number of members that maintain hugely fulfilling careers in the NHS.

For all healthcare professionals in their efforts to safeguard the NHS and continually improve services.

Gillian Hooper

Overcoming Selective Blindness

Improving Services from
the Bedside to the
Boardroom and Beyond

Austin Macauley Publishers™
LONDON • CAMBRIDGE • NEW YORK • SHARJAH

Copyright © Gillian Hooper 2023

The right of Gillian Hooper to be identified as author of this work has been asserted by the author in accordance with sections 77 and 78 of the Copyright, Designs and Patents Act 1988.

All rights reserved. No part of this publication may be reproduced, stored in a retrieval system, or transmitted in any form or by any means, electronic, mechanical, photocopying, recording, or otherwise, without the prior permission of the publishers.

Any person who commits any unauthorised act in relation to this publication may be liable to criminal prosecution and civil claims for damages.

A CIP catalogue record for this title is available from the British Library.

ISBN 9781035843947 (Paperback)
ISBN 9781035843954 (ePub e-book)

www.austinmacauley.com

First Published 2023
Austin Macauley Publishers Ltd®
1 Canada Square
Canary Wharf
London
E14 5AA

It has been an absolute privilege for me to have worked within so many differing organisations and alongside so many outstanding individuals over recent years, with the common goal of improving services for patients. I have enjoyed more than I could possibly have imagined the stimulation and satisfaction born from working in this way and for being reminded how fortunate the NHS is to have such an impressive cadre of committed experts working within it to make sure it thrives for the generation that follows us.

Although there have been too many inspiring individuals, impressive senior leadership teams and organisations to acknowledge specifically, there is one organisation that I do wish to specifically recognise – Worcestershire Acute Hospitals NHS Trust. I began working with this trust in 2017, when the organisation was viewed as being in the deep dark trench of special measures. The range of commendable initiatives and efforts consistently made by the senior leadership team across this trust, and the openness to considering alternative ways of approaching how to sustainably improve services was humbling. They embraced some of the principles conveyed within this book with hope and enthusiasm, particularly focusing on implementing the seven levels of operational assurance framework and translating them locally in a way that was authentic and bespoke to their local circumstances. They appreciated the insights that independent reviews could offer them and in due course turned their attention to strengthening the effectiveness of their sub-committees. Achieving this all whilst key individuals left, new colleagues joined and priorities around the trust continued to evolve. The trust's improvement was so significant the chief inspector for hospitals recommended in 2019 that the trust be removed from special measures regime. Whilst this is an achievement worthy of acknowledgement, so also is the behaviour of this trust in terms of its ongoing commitment to proactively share its experiential learning with others. I am both indebted and grateful to the individuals who have personally championed the approaches recommended within this book. They have been an inspiration and continue to be an absolute pleasure to work alongside.

Table of Contents

Chapter 1: Why Is This Book Needed?	13
Chapter 2: Characteristics of 'High Performing' Organisations	31
Chapter 3: Characteristics of 'Struggling' Organisations	40
Chapter 4: Assessing an Organisation's Potential for Improvement	46
Chapter 5: An Effective Framework for Assuring Improvement	56
Chapter 6: SMART 'Plus' Action/Improvement Plans	68
Chapter 7: Root-Cause-Analysis (RCA)	85
Chapter 8: Developing Internal Independence	101
Chapter 9: Seven Steps to Operational Assurance	116
Chapter 10: Defining Strategic Assurance Levels	126
Chapter 11: Effective Committee Working	140
Chapter 12: Eradicating Selective Blindness Across the NHS	149

Chapter 1
Why Is This Book Needed?

I have frequently experienced that it can be extremely difficult for good people to do the right thing. I come from a large family of good people: more than a fair share of who have enjoyed lifelong careers in the NHS. Over the decades we have shared our frustrations and aspirations with each other regarding the failings and potential of the NHS. We have forensically argued the merits of general management, the risks of introducing clinical directorships, the necessity of commissioning, the impact of political influence driven by the goal of retaining control of parliamentary seats and more recently why there exists such a flexible use of the term 'new build' when referring to a hospital. These discussions were usually held around the dinner table, replicating many similar discussions held within families where individuals with different knowledge and experiences have differing perspectives on issues; my family having more than a few heated debates of what needs to be done to resuscitate an ailing NHS. Individually, each of us who has trained or worked in the NHS for any substantial length of time has developed a wider 'family' consisting of a substantial network of similarly experienced NHS colleagues with whom we have explored or mutual frustrations regarding the limitations of our ability to make a difference and our individual spheres of influence. These members of our family, our friends and our colleagues always ready to offer practical or emotional support in any way possible as they understand only too well that there has never been any doubt that each of us passionately love the NHS and despite everything that we might view as failing within it, we are proud to be a part of it. As a clinician in any profession, the job satisfaction one gets from working with 'patients' is phenomenal. I've always felt rather sorry for those who work in other fields and industries as I'm sure that no other job could possible even begin to come close to comparing to being a clinician. To have the opportunity of supporting and making a difference to the experience and outcomes of individual 'patients' when they often are at their most vulnerable is amazingly humbling. It inspires one to offer a level of personalisation and compassion that one would hope for if one found oneself in a similar situation. The gratitude from individuals is often immediate; always authentic and heartfelt. The motivation that is generated by the relationship formed between clinician and 'patient' to consistently replicate this level of intervention is high. Despite huge frustrations with some roles, I held during my clinical career, I could never identify any other role that could even hope to come close to offering the day-to-day levels of job satisfaction that nursing could, so I willingly stayed with it, specialised and moved into professional and corporate management and then more strategic national positions with the aspiration of continuing to increase my sphere of influence even further.

The Need to Support Inexperience:

I would love to think that I might have achieved great things in the first board position that I held but in truth, I simply began to learn how essential it was to survive at this level by effectively navigating the challenges of developing myself as a professional leader within a politically (With a small p) charged corporate environment. The aspects of this role that came easily to me, were those rooted in my clinical or professional knowledge base. Other aspects I found to be considerably trickier to make any progress with this despite my good intentions, organisational commitment and work ethic. For those of you with whom this dynamic might resonate, you might understand if I say that I fervently hoped colleagues might choose to focus on the positive aspects of any legacy I left, rather than dwell too long on the many intractable issues with which despite my best endeavours I'd seemed to have made little discernible progress during my time with the trust. So why was I unable to 'do the right thing' in this role where I seemed to have the legitimate authority to do so? In this scenario, I was hugely inexperienced and made an obvious rookie error. I had demonstrated an unhelpful degree of 'selective blindness' in very simply and naively failing to recognise or understand the strength of the local culture. I had focused my efforts towards developing strategies, systems and processes, which others far wiser than I, could easily see would be eaten for breakfast by the pervading culture of the organisation. This example offering us the first legitimate reason for selective blindness and good people not doing the right thing in the NHS; the age old one of inexperience.

The Need to Transfer Specialist Knowledge:

Dusting myself off and chalking this up to experience, my resolve as I transitioned into a larger and more clinically complex trust was to work harder, faster, longer in my new role, to ensure that I could increase the impact and potential to achieve in this role. The scale of the organisation's intractable issues and the political reality of being part of a leadership team within a community representing several marginal parliamentary seats took considerable capacity and capability to navigate without too much damage to self, colleagues or the organisation. Long story short, I was required as an add-on to my extensive portfolio to assume responsibility for a fixed period of time for an area I had no significant experience in: meeting all A&E targets. With five years of board experience under my belt, I enthusiastically forged good relationships with the local ambulance service and carved out considerable time to work alongside staff who were exasperated with increasing queue of ambulances, delayed assessment and treatment times for patients. I supported the implementation of a number of initiatives that colleagues believed would alleviate the pressures being experienced on a daily basis. Despite this herculean effort and some commendable successes in other areas of my portfolio, I failed to achieve any discernible progress in the achievement of A&E targets. The reason for this not becoming apparent to me until sometime later after I had left the organisation to take up a new national improvement role where I gained a forensic knowledge of capacity and demand and understanding for the first time how queues form! This delayed insight brought me shame as I realised that despite my best efforts, good intentions and hard work, I had again been thwarted by my own selective blindness making it impossible to make any progress. The theory of queues, how they form and how to best reduce the waiting experience within them is as I'm sure many of you will appreciate, alarmingly straightforward. However, if one doesn't have this level of understanding and has responsibility for queues of any description, one can with the best of intentions instigate a range of initiatives aimed at reducing queues that do indeed compound rather than relieve the situation. Some of the techniques to measure the effectiveness of initiatives in place to manage and reduce queue times can require a little more explanation but it certainly isn't rocket science. This example offering us a second legitimate reason for individual selective blindness and experienced good people not doing the right thing in the NHS; the age old one that affects us all at some point in our career path, that relating to an absence of specialist knowledge.

Leading a team of experts to work directly with trusts to improve performance of access targets was where the penny began to drop for me and for the first time in my career, I wrote an article 'Trust Building Measures'[1], which reflected on my experience of working within the Modernisation Agency and what I considered to be the lost opportunity of achieving and sustaining widespread improvements across the NHS through transferring the capability held within that organisation to trusts on a greater scale.

As I gained experience and specialist knowledge, I transitioned into increasingly more complex roles in commissioning, the department of health, the London Deanery and Health Education England (HEE). However, in each one of these positions, I experienced a similar realisation, reflecting that if I had acquired earlier in my career the specialist knowledge considered to be rudimentary in each newly acquired position, how much more effective I could have been in my previous role. For example, if I had been appointed to my secondary care roles with even a rudimentary insight into what motivated primary care teams, I could have been so much more effective in engage with them to develop improved patient focused pathways of care. Similarly, as a director challenged with finding solutions to intractable problems at the coal face, with a very limited appreciation of how to connect with and influence the expertise available within the department of health, I was unable to access the range of expert knowledge and support potentially available to optimise the impact I could make. Later, when I landed the role at the London Deanery in part due to the extent of my previous collaborative working with medical colleagues, I was stunned at the scale of my ignorance regarding the complexities of post graduate medical education. Considering the degree of corporate responsibilities held by myself in previous roles within organisations where the provision of post graduate medical education was germane to the delivery of all services, it was not surprising that I felt further shame regarding my obvious limitations. This reoccurring cyclical dynamic being at best frustrating given the unavailable solution to undertake one's career path in reverse!

The Need to Increase one's Sphere of Influence:

The dynamic described above, the frustration of wishing that one could draw upon knowledge and experience only available later in your career path to optimise one's impact in one's current role, is one of the drivers for me writing this book now. Wishing to disrupt this dynamic I am attempting to capture the learning and best practice identified over the last decade, for your consideration and benefit to potentially increase your own effectiveness, job satisfaction and ultimately your own sphere of influence. There is too much that needs to be achieved across the NHS for us to keep replicating the pattern of the past and for good people to keep reinventing the wheel in order to move forward. As I can personally attest to the drive for one to increase one's own sphere of influence to be as strong at the outset of one's career as it is towards the end of one's career, the potential impact of transferring the learning from one individual to another does not diminish over time.

The shared learning within these pages presents the two factors of inexperience and lack of specialist knowledge to be the easiest of the factors to address within oneself when considering selective blindness as a reason for good people not doing the right things. It is a certainty that these factors are present to an extent in each of us. The practical aspects in this book, the descriptors of best practice and the opportunities identified for strengthening the focus, momentum and sustainability of improvements are offered as a pragmatic and safe option for individuals at any level and in any role in a trust to strengthen what they are doing now. This book also seeks to explore the trickier scenario whereby selective blindness is recognised as being present in others, often in those of considerable seniority holding positions of significant legitimate power and influence and often employed in organisations external to our own. However, rather than accepting the 'politics' of such a scenario as completely beyond one's ability to influence, these same tools and techniques suggested to increase the pace and sustainability of improvements at a local and individual level, may be equally impactful when utilised to establish an irrefutable evidential base from which one may increase ones influence of in a position to influence beyond our own organisational boundaries towards the wider NHS.

The Need to Translate Organisational Learning:

In 2013, I was very honoured to be invited by the CQC's first ever appointed Chief Inspector for Hospitals to act as one of only two non-medical independent chairs for the comprehensive trust wide regulatory inspections being undertaken. This was a wonderful opportunity for me that began my transition to establishing a portfolio of positions and working independently with senior leadership teams. So, for the last decade I have worked in a variety of capacities; always with the aim of supporting healthcare organisations to improve aspects of service provision that may be sustained over time, this aiming to serve as a bed-rock for organisational transformation.

Some organisations I have worked with in this capacity over a period of years; some for just a few weeks or months at a time. Always aiming to authentically engage with a cross section of staff to collaboratively develop and deliver improvement plans to address long standing issues of significant concern. In many organisations, I have simply been a member of a wider team undertaking a regulatory inspection or undertaking an external audit of a location or specialty, providing evidenced findings and recommendations for the organisation to hopefully adopt and address. All these ways of working have allowed me to develop a deep understanding of effective methods of evaluating service provision and have informed the aspect of work I have most enjoyed and that I believe has been of most value to organisations; significantly increasing the extent to which organisations not only deliver improvement plans in place but more importantly achieve and sustain the described outcomes being sought.

Time and time again, I have worked with organisations who genuinely believe they have delivered all aspects of an agreed improvement plan only for the Care Quality Commission (CQC) to inspect and present further evidence of ongoing concerns and persistent variation in standards. An organisational degree of selective blindness is born from inexperience or lack of specialist knowledge and often a range of other contributing factors that may or may not be relatively straightforward to address. This frustrating and cyclical dynamic can not only create huge personal disappointment and fear for some individuals regarding their own security of employment but also often results in widespread organisational consternation and disbelief with significant emotional efforts channelled into challenging evidence prior to varying degrees of eventual acceptance/compliance. There is a degree of inevitably in the extent of pressure exerted from external stakeholders for the production of usually another 'action plan', with this new plan often required to be significantly more detailed than the last and accompanied with additional layers of 'oversight' established to provide assurance to local stakeholders of real time progress. I have seen this dynamic replicated again and again, often frustratingly with limited personal success in influencing the powers that be that insisting on more and more detail of intended plans only serves to generate unfounded reassurance that progress will indeed now be made. This compounded by an increasing confusion of the senior leadership team, unable to understand why despite doing everything asked of them and the considerable focus and efforts that had been made, improvements had not been realised with nothing significant changing for staff, patients or service users. In such a scenario, the organisation's commendable effort to overcome its own degree of selective blindness usually through steps taken to strengthening the capacity and capability of the senior leadership team, can have the effect of exposing the selective blindness evident in some of their key stakeholders representing other parts of the system. This example is offering us a third and final legitimate reason for selective blindness effecting experienced and knowledgeable good people not doing the right thing in the NHS; the trickiest of the issues to address, where the selective blindness is evident externally and fuelled by fear and futility.

The Need to 'Feel the Fear and Do It Anyway':

Unlike many with the pressures of relentless new priorities and the weight of accountability on their shoulders, I have found myself for the first time in my NHS career with the luxury of sufficient time to truly reflect upon each experience to ensure that this informs the next approach I take with an organisation. This allowing me to develop greater clarity each time of the levers and actions that will have the most impact. Perhaps more importantly I have also increased the degree to which I have been able to transfer capability to an organisation or individuals. Being personally free of any corporate responsibility from being a member of a trust board and the inevitable constraints this can engender has offered me a truly wonderful opportunity to create a safe space for colleagues to explore and consider if what they are being asked to do or are expected to do is indeed what is needed and what will support sustainable improvement and transformation of services where required. It has offered the exploration of an alternative ways of doing things. An approach that presents not only no risk of any description to individuals but of even greater value, an often-unique opportunity to identify individual's knowledge and experience gaps, allowing these to be explored and addressed to create local solutions to their specific problems.

The Need to Identify the Correct Solution to a Problem:

I have made the decision that the luxury of my position will also extend to attempting to call out the selective blindness of others who hold offices that directly influence and impact upon the performance of trusts. I have observed many of these individuals seeming to demonstrate a limited appreciation of the significance of the role they undertake, or in any range of matters attempting to behave and operate to reflect the standards they seek from others, particularly those who work in trusts. There seem to be an increasing number of media reports from these individuals in higher office, regarding the solutions that they wish to see in place to address long standing performance concerns across the NHS. These solutions being so inappropriate that they would appear to evidence an extreme degree of selective blindness in the individual the cause of which being inexperience, lack of specialist knowledge or potentially something more challenging relating to the politics of needing to be seen to be taking action which (they must realise) is unlikely to have any positive impact at all. As an example of the latter cause, one of our recent potential prime ministers wanted us to believe that charging people failing to turn up for scheduled GP appointments was a solution that would improve the efficiency and effectiveness of primary care. This suggestion will be recognised by the vast majority of those working in the NHS as nothing short of nonsense and not considered to be a solution to anything! If in the (unlikely) event that it was truly considered to be a potential solution to the GP access problem, then we need urgently to call out this unacceptable level of selective blindness held by an individual at this level. One might hope that presenting the some of the evidence such as the lead time of 28 days for scheduling an appointment, the limitations in being able to change or cancel these appointments and the rationale for not proactively factoring into booking systems an inevitable and indeed desirable level of non-attendance, might assist in providing the required education. Similarly, a Health Secretary seemed to think that the issue of ambulance turnaround times will be solved by recruiting more call handlers and a new IT system. Again, even if there are a small number of ambulance trusts whose performance might be improved with more call handlers this initiative wont impact turnaround times because the cause of ambulance waiting times isn't affected to any degree by the time taken to answer the call centre phone! Proposing the implementation of a new IT system being quite simply a solution to a different problem. Recognising the need to improve ambulance turnaround times at A&E departments, one must acknowledge the difficulties corporate directors might have in responding to requirements to reorganise triage arrangements, provide incentives to increase specialist medical assessments, establish operational protocols to recognise the flexible walls of A&E departments etc. Whilst it is possible there are trusts where such initiatives might have real impact on improving the flow of patients through the hospital and therefore the turnaround times of ambulances, it is most likely that the majority of trusts directors expected to drive these improvements will know that such initiatives are only being directed towards the symptom of the problem, not the cause. One must acknowledge and recognise the personal risk to any individual considering to decline invitations to initiate such efforts; knowing that to achieve the outcomes being sought and a sustainable solution to the problem, one should focus on the extent of current NHS information evidencing the barn door obvious 'root cause' of this situation being any problem with accessing the front door of a hospital being directly linked to the ability to open the back door to facilitate an exit. This directly related to reducing the ever increasing number of patients in acute beds as they wait a transfer to an intermediate care or social care facility. This very recognisable situational example highlights the concept of external selective blindness, which I feel will resonate with even for those new to the NHS, hence featuring in the title of this book.

The Need to Recognise the Widespread Existence of Blind Spots:

Selective blindness can present in us all – we all will have limitations of experience and gaps in specialist knowledge. We will all have bias and prejudices that can distort our perception of issues and contribute to blind spots. In the absence of an appetite to overcome individual selective blindness, selective blindness can grow and take hold across an organisation, which we will explore when we look at struggling organisations. Whilst there may be a few who resist change and are steadfast in their view of the world, most individuals I have worked with are grateful for a safe space to explore alternatives and welcome the opportunity to learn, improve their working practice and ultimately increase their personal sphere of influence. Only in taking this approach to address any individual selective blindness or internal selective blindness within an organisation can the leaders in such an organisation position themselves to call out and demand that selective blindness present in their stakeholders is also addressed. In my experience, the most damaging effects are seen when selective blindness is present within an external stakeholder to an organisation. In this scenario, selective blindness can eat up those rare NHS resources of clinical capacity and expert capability, directing them pointlessly towards symptoms of variation because to recognise the root cause is considered too difficult or politically unacceptable.

The Need to Recognise How Assurance Drives Improvement:

During 2017 and 2018, the CQC published reports of how NHS acute trusts and NHS mental health trusts had achieved significant improvements in their ratings[2]. These reports evidenced that self-evaluation, assurance and accreditation were at the heart of continuous improvement, with a growing number of improvement projects in each trust requiring robust assurance and risk management processes. The approach described in this book to achieving sustainable improvements through strengthening assurance processes has made a significant difference to trusts grappling with distilling and focusing priorities, helping to build momentum to address systemic causes of variation.

Working alongside so many experienced committed individuals and teams in the capacity of critical friend where I have continued to learn as much as I have supported others to learn, has honestly been the most rewarding experience of my career to date and certainly the most enjoyable. I have considered it an honour to be able to focus wholly upon building both the capability and confidence of individuals and leadership teams, concentrating on identifying what the root cause of any variation is and in strengthening their approach to effectively improving services. This has been both motivating and hugely rewarding. The relationship formed have provided some head space to identify and focus on the systemic causes of variations rather than the initially identified concerns and developed small steps towards curing the levels of selective blindness all too often present in the system. In turn, this can create an opportunity to reduce the reliance on the opinions of others regarding what improvement should be prioritised and taken forward, supporting colleagues in taking back control of determining local priorities for improving local standards. Playing a small part in rebuilding the confidence of hard working committed NHS colleagues and the positive impact this has on motivation and self-belief has been a totally unexpected gift for me which has been a very personal motivator to step out of my own comfort zone, stick my head above the parapet and attempt to write a book to offer this opportunity more widely to others.

I am confident that there would be little argument with the belief that key to organisations reducing variation, consistently achieving desired standards and setting their own local priorities for improvement is the need for there to be strong and consistent internal assurance processes embedded across every part of the organisation. Working directly with a relatively small number of trusts that have found themselves deep in special measures for prolonged periods of time has enabled me to develop an explicit stepped approach to generating robust assurance at a 'micro' operational level which provides an opportunity for greater local control. This creating a firm path of continual improvement and a basis of generating robust assurance of progress. This approach which has been developed and tested is detailed in forthcoming chapters, using experiential learning from each organisation and best practice from the independent sector. Without fail every organisation that has adopted elements of this approach has significantly strengthened the grip, pace and sustainability of improvement being sought; with all the organisations demonstrably improving over time. With growing evidence that this approach works, I have as stated, been motivated to attempt to write this book to potentially share more widely and offer something to any organisation regardless of their track record or current regulatory rating. I am motivated to try to short circuit the route by which experience, information and knowledge can be available to help individuals responsible for hugely complex portfolios increase their effectiveness in their current roles. Whether you be a clinician asked to develop or deliver an action plan, a governance facilitator asked to oversee improvement for a specific area, an executive director charged with providing assurance of progress to colleagues, a non-executive director seeking assurance of delivery, or a stakeholder required to form an independent view of an organisations progress, this short easily digestible self-help book will absolutely provide some practical options for improving the impact of the approach you have taken thus far by substantially helping you to call out and overcome selective blindness that may be hindering improvement across your organisation. When you have optimised your approach to improving services, you will find that you have a firm platform for increasing your influence with your stakeholders and identifying and addressing any degree of external selective blindness that currently prevents you and your organisation from delivering the quality of services your patients deserve.

The Need for Practical Help Now:

The following chapters invite you to take a fresh look at your current organisations' approach to identify those elements that might have best impact for your local situation. Regardless of your current performance and degree of confidence in your local arrangements, the chapters will provide you with the tools to overcome any degree of selective blindness that may be present. Only when this is achieved locally will you be able credibly look wider across to your stakeholders and external partners to demand the same from them. These same tools and techniques offering a safe, evidence based and constructive approach to engaging across organisational boundaries to sustainably improve services. I hope you will enjoy and embrace how you could increase the impact of the efforts you are making locally to achieve the improvements you are seeking and rise to the challenge of seeking the same externally from others. If we are able to achieve this in sufficient numbers, then also working collaboratively we will be able to ensure that the NHS can continue to improve and remain as our much-loved institution.

Chapter 2
Characteristics of 'High Performing' Organisations

Before we dive into describing the practicalities of establishing a strong assurance framework, I would like us to pause and consider the many and varied ways of recognising 'high performing' organisations. In my experience, whatever the route by which one comes into contact with an organisation, as a patient, potential employee or as a colleague, one is able to recognise very quickly the visual or behavioural clues that make one notice those experiences that suggest high performance. In highlighting the characteristic that I have consistently observed in the organisations I have worked with over the last ten years that have been formally recognised as performing well, my intention is to stimulate the act of self-assessment within the reader. The organisations I am drawing upon all operating within a wide range of differing sectors, demographical, financial and environmental scenarios.

Subliminal Messages

Firstly, some initial thoughts on coming into contact with high performing organisations. I'm sure we can all relate to the subliminal messages conveyed by the environment of something as basic as a reception area and how these can significantly evoke feelings of both confidence and concern. Subliminal messages often so influential in forming judgements about all manner of aspects of service delivery, culture and expectations influence us all equally, whether we are a visitor, service users or members of a regulatory inspection team. The equivalent of the initial impression made by a patient entering a reception area, for an inspection team is the briefing material made available to the team prior to the inspection taking place. The calibre of the preparatory documentation provided by trusts to brief inspection teams provides an early litmus test that most certainly influences the approach planned to be taken by the team. Equally, an external auditor will view the clarity of an action plan as offering the bedrock for a fair assessment and the potential to demonstrate progress. In terms of how the organisation connects with others, a trust adopting a proactive organisational approach to securing independent support to address issues of concern, can indicate an impressive appetite and openness to learn and improve that can positively inform the view of the leadership team before a single conversation may have taken place. The means by which first impressions are formed and the importance of the associated subliminal messages should not be underestimated.

More specifically though, having engaged with trusts from every sector, acute, community, integrated, mental health, specialist and ambulance, I have consistently observed a number of characteristics that are readily found in the very highest performing organisations. I share these below with a short explanation simply to encourage some initial self-reflection in the reader regarding their view of their own organisations position upon the continuum from 'good to great'.

Responding to the Unexpected

Often the first characteristic that becomes noticeable relates to how the organisation responds to the unexpected. Whether this be an unannounced inspection, an incident of some kind or simply an unexpected audit or review being undertaken; in such events, I have without exception found the individuals within organisations take such events in their stride, ensuring any disruption is swiftly responded to, enabling routine business to seamlessly return to normal with minimum pause or distraction. Such organisations are always recognised as high performing. In such organisations, the senior leadership team has the confidence and approach to genuinely influence their regulators; in term of frequency and nature of dialogue, inspections scheduled, and effectiveness of interventions and reviews undertaken. They are confident they know their business and demonstrate perseverance in evidencing this to others.

Leadership Culture

Similarly early conversations with leaders convey those senior leaders across the organisation see themselves as 'servants' of their workforce, with multiple examples easily identified that demonstrate genuine engagement and understanding underpins decisions taken at all levels within the organisation. Linked with this characteristic is the evidence of strong personal relationships formed across multiple levels within an organisation, from ward to board, supporting the safe exploration and challenge required for individuals and teams to authentically influence decisions taken and demonstrate humility. Genuine humility being such a tricky quality to describe or evidence and certainly not mentioned in any CQC Key Line of Enquiry (KLOE)[3] but one that is so extremely easy to recognise. I can recall many examples when faced with an individual describing the delivery of what is so clearly outstanding clinical or managerial practice, noting that their focus was not being on expecting to receive recognition for this, but rather more humbly firmly directed upon describing their intentions and need to further improve. Without exception, when working as a regulator, I found when feeding back to trusts that they are to be rated 'OUTSTANDING', they expressed genuine shock at receiving this recognition, their explanation of their shock being because there is simply so much more they wish to achieve. This leadership response being in marked contrast to the number of organisations who have expressed profound disappointment at being recognised as rated 'GOOD', often feeling that this failed to recognise sufficiently that which individuals within the organisation considered to be and expected to be externally recognised as outstanding.

Clear Governance Arrangements

If one references the CQC's descriptors of outstanding ratings, one can summarise all high performing organisations as demonstrating an absolute clarity on responsibilities, portfolios, operational and governance decision making arrangements, with demonstrable tried and tested improvements over time and the learning from failures and successes widely recognised and familiar to staff. That is not to say that all systems and processes are optimum in these trusts, but that there is a clarity and transparency regarding arrangements that means all staff at every level know how information is generated, synthesized and interpreted to promote improvement. Regular review and an openness to continually develop and improve data, information and decision making are central to all governance activities, which involve a wide range of individuals from differing professions, teams and levels across the whole organisation.

Specifically, the CQC's detailed definitions of 'outstanding' include reference to:

- Leaders having a deep understanding of issues, challenges and priorities in their service.
- There being a systematic and integrated approach to monitoring, reviewing and providing evidence of progress against the strategy and plans. Plans being also consistently implemented and impacting positively on quality and sustainability of services.
- Strong collaboration, team-working and support across all functions and a common focus on improving the quality and sustainability of care and people's experiences.
- Governance arrangements that are proactively reviewed to reflect best practice.
- Evidence of consistently high levels of constructive engagement with staff and people who use services, the public and stakeholders which is seen as a vital way of holding services to account.

- A fully embedded and systematic approach to improvement, making consistent use of a recognised improvement methodology.

Focusing again upon behaviours, in my experience what one observes in outstanding trusts is that there are locally explicit professional clinical and managerial standards, staff are proud of these, and these behaviours are consistently displayed. Staff are confident, are energised and enjoy their work. Senior leaders give importance to deeply explaining their local approach and priorities to others, as they want colleagues to fully understand local challenges and achievements. External stakeholders, inspectors, consultants are inspired by this culture and themselves express "This is somewhere I'd like to work".

So, a key question for you is what if any of these characteristics and reflections resonate with your current organisation? It is hoped that offering these experiential observations of outstanding organisations provides the stimulus for some early identification of aspects you would wish to see developed in your own current organisation, providing some important context to inform a later focus on governance and assurance arrangements. If, however you are confident that by any measure your organisation would be considered outstanding and consider it unlikely that you might find anything of significant value within these pages; I would wish to challenge that viewpoint, assuring you that there will be. The recognition that high performing organisations have clear and transparent governance arrangements that are widely understood by staff, does not preclude the potential for these governance arrangements to be further developed. In coming pages, we will explore the potential for every organisation to strengthen its governance arrangements in a range of simple and practical ways in addition to encouraging the exploration of the presence of selective blindness within individuals in key positions, specific teams or possibly the entire organisation in some regard. The existence of selective blindness significantly effects the improvements that can be realised by any organisation. The challenge for a truly outstanding team, service or trust with embedded best practice processes for improving services will be not only to maintain the exacting regulatory standards described in part above but more importantly to seek to increase their sphere of influence externally. This being, in my observation by far the most challenging, as it requires the courage of individual leaders to call out and overcome selective blindness present in colleagues who are often in positions of greater seniority or external stakeholders, which undoubtedly is associated with the greatest degree of individual risk and fear.

Chapter Summary

Characteristics of High Performing Organisations

1. No pause or distraction – these organisations take unexpected events in their stride, recovering quickly, returning swiftly to business as usual.
2. Leaders see themselves as 'servants' of their workforce – engagement and understanding underpinning decision making at all levels.
3. Humility, humility, humility – regardless of the outstanding clinical practice that may be provided the attention is on improving further rather than gaining recognition.
4. Strong personal relationships – from ward to Board ideal.
5. Absolute clarity on responsibilities, portfolios, operational and governance arrangements.
6. Tried and tested improvements over time – learning from failures and successes are recognised and familiar to staff.
7. Exemplary behaviours consistently displayed – staff are proud of explicit professional clinical and managerial standards.
8. Staff are confidence, have energy and enjoy their work – visitors, external stakeholders, inspectors express "This is somewhere I'd like to work".
9. Leaders give importance to deeply explaining their local approach and priorities to stakeholders; they want colleagues to fully understand local challenges and achievements.
10. They have genuinely influenced their regulators – in term of frequency and nature of dialogue, inspections scheduled, effectiveness of interventions and reviews undertaken.

> This self-help guide has a great deal to offer all organisations regardless of their existing recognised performance. As the improvement potential of every organisation can be limited by the internal presence of selective blindness or more challenging the presence of selective blindness in external stakeholders which can require considerable courage to attempt to overcome.

Chapter 3
Characteristics of 'Struggling' Organisations

In contrast, the common characteristics that I have experientially observed in trusts identified as needing significant support to improve the quality-of-service provision and overall performance are interestingly not simply the opposite of those found in high performing organisations as outlined earlier. It's therefore helpful for us to consider these issues prior to beginning to explore in detail the relatively simple opportunities there are for strengthening the differing approaches being taken locally to improving services.

Challenge and Denial

Regardless of the nature of the role I have adopted in engaging with struggling organisations, I have without fail experienced these as focusing significant and often protracted energies on forensically examining the detail of issues whilst comprehensively failing to recognise or acknowledge the bigger picture. This often evidenced by the prolonged challenging of draft reports, questioning accuracy and denying evidence provided by external parties, often accompanied with considerable disbelief voiced at the perceived inadequacies of external independent findings and recommendations. In short, in such organisations you are likely to come across individuals in key leadership positions who themselves display a profound and deep-seated condition of selective blindness, for which it can be very difficult for colleagues to challenge. Unfortunately, such a response primarily has the effect of delaying finalisation and any formal organisational consideration of the information available, which in turn has a detrimental effect on the timeliness of the organisational response required to begin to address concerns raised. This approach whilst possibly is reinforcing an organisational belief that they have rightly challenged points of accuracy or detail, always makes the task of addressing organisational issues successfully more challenging due to the delay in taking any positive action. In simple terms, this is the equivalent of shooting oneself in the foot before commencing a 100-metre sprint. I have often reflected that this all-too-common response is a consequence of geographical or professional isolation experienced by the organisation and the leaders within it. In such circumstances, the exploration of strategic alliances focused towards expanding the professional and experiential horizon of the leaders within the organisation can prove to be transformative in swiftly addressing the experiential and knowledge-based causes of selective blindness that has so significantly affected the historical effectiveness of the leadership team to date. Gaps/interims around the board table can also often present a challenge to organisational memory, with further key capacity and capability gaps presenting significant limitations to establishing the strategic and operational response required to begin to develop a plan to address issues. These behaviours and issues all serving to delay identifying and addressing the often-longstanding systemic issues, whilst giving a misleading impression of engagement and activity.

Isolation

When engaging with staff across a struggling organisation, one can often observe a widespread and marked disinterest in how others do thing, both internally within other teams or divisions and externally within other organisations. This behaviour often contributes to an absence of a critical mass to be found within the organisation that knows or can describe what 'good' looks like. Without such a critical mass, the pace of any progress will inevitably be set by a minority of highly motivated individuals working in isolation and therefore be glacially slow. Multiple examples of an absence of genuine clinical engagement can also usually be identified in these organisations, with junior doctors in training often described as a 'lost tribe', with colleagues not knowing who they are, what they do or who they work for. These behaviours and issues all contributing to an impenetrable barrier to effective engagement with staff across the organisation for the benefit of patients and the delivery of high-quality services.

No Clear Strategic Narrative

In direct contrary to high performing organisations, in all struggling organisations one finds an absence of a cohesive strategic narrative regarding quality priorities. The absence of explicit strategic priorities means the importance of potential improvements are not able to be evaluated in term of their significance, or their to achieving strategic objectives, resulting in all potential improvement initiatives being given the same degree of importance and focus. Struggling trusts may often have numerous different action plans in operation but usually no comprehensive overarching organisation wide improvement plan, this leading to considerable efforts being made towards individual action plan delivery, with a fractured overview of the organisational impact of improvement activity. Without fail, in all such trusts there can be found general widespread confusion regarding all aspects of governance arrangements and which in turn and without exception generates a primary internal focus on reassurance rather than assurance.

Ineffective Performance Management

Compared with the culture often described in high performing organisations, the most significant cultural aspect of struggling organisations with the characteristics described above can often be summarised as there being no consequence of deficient performance. Appointing the most able strategic leaders in such organisations is critically important. Allowing the culture required of the organisation to be described, engendered, and conveyed by those at the very top of the organisation, establishes the environment necessary to support grip, momentum, and sustainability of improvements. Being appointed to leadership positions in struggling organisations has not tended to be seen as an attractive or desirable career option. Organisations that have been recognised as having serious failures in quality of care requiring 'special measures' or what has been launched in July 2021 as the national Recovery Support programme

(RSP)[4] may have experienced many years of discrete decline and concern prior to their performance being confirmed in such a manner. It is not possible for such a scenario to be reversed swiftly but also not possible in the absence of a critical mass of like-minded individuals appointed permanently to leadership positions at every level across the organisation. It has taken too long for this need to attract the strongest of individuals to lead these organisations to be recognised with only recently the importance of this being voiced nationally.

I have no doubt that aspects of the characteristics described above will resonate to an extent with every reader; with many having worked at some point within such organisations. Whilst at the time of writing, there are currently 15 organisations in the Recovery Support programme, representing seven of the regions and five of the newly formed Integrated Care Boards also identified as requiring intensive support, it is hoped that the impact of the support available to these organisations to establish sustainable capability to improve services, will ensure that the number of such organisations will decrease over time. It is likely that many of us working within trusts not formally identified as part of the RSP, will remain able to recognise sections of our organisations that display some elements of these characteristics and as such effect the full potential being realised of the organisation. The aspects of denial, disengagement, a focus on symptomatic issues and failure to hold others to account all evidencing the potential existence of selective blindness present at differing levels throughout the organisation and in some instances evident across entire organisations. Hold these issues in your mind as we go on to consider a simple framework for assessing an organisation's potential to improve and begin to identify a number of straightforward ways of seeking to reduce and mitigate the effects of selective blindness where evident within an organisation.

Chapter Summary

Characteristics of Struggling Organisations

1. Challenge to reports, denial, disbelief.
2. Isolation – geographical/professional. Disinterest in how others do things.
3. Lack of clinical engagement.
4. No critical mass of knowing what 'good' looks like.
5. Confusion regarding governance arrangements.
6. A focus on reassurance rather than assurance.
7. Absence of a strategic narrative regarding quality priorities.
8. No clear improvement plan, organisational approach, addressing systemic issues.
9. Key capacity and capability gaps, strategic, operational and improvement orientated.
10. Culture where there are no consequences of poor performance.

Often in these organisations you can find an unhelpful degree of selective blindness within individuals and in some instances across the whole organisation. A critical mass of like-minded leaders, appointed permanently and given support over time to improve services and being required to sustain any improvements in these organisations.

Chapter 4
Assessing an Organisation's Potential for Improvement

So having begun to reflect upon the extreme range of organisational performance and how the characteristics identified might resonate with your own current organisation, we can begin to explore how regardless of the recognised performance of the organisation, one may form a view of the organisation's potential to improve.

Through my engagement with multiple trusts in a variety of different roles, my initial judgement of a trust's potential for driving sustainable improvement has been informed using a simple assessment framework. This framework able to be used equally effectively to assess the potential for the organisation as a whole or a defined element of the organisation such as a specific team, a specialism or services sharing a given location. As such this framework offers an easy route for any individual wishing to assess the potential for the ward they work on, the multidisciplinary team they are a member of or the organisation they are considering joining. In essence, this framework seeks evidence of the extent to which a clinical area, specialist team or trust can demonstrate it has:

- A firm grip of both urgent and important issues.
- The necessary pace and momentum of work to address issues.
- Evidence of sustained improvement over time.

The framework frames four key questions relevant for any area, team or organisation regardless of existing performance, sector or size. The framework seeks to assess the extent to which an area, team or trust can respond positively to these four areas of enquiry. This framework is summarised below, prior to each of the four questions being explored in detail at an organisational level.

An Organisational Framework for Improvement:

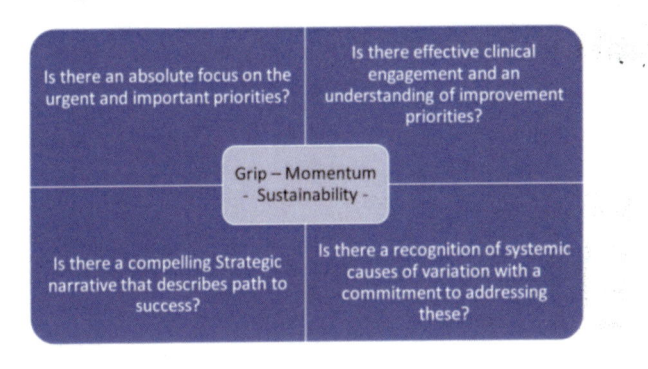

Is there an absolute focus on the urgent and important priorities?	Is there effective clinical engagement and an understanding of improvement priorities?
Grip – Momentum - Sustainability -	
Is there a compelling Strategic narrative that describes path to success?	Is there a recognition of systemic causes of variation with a commitment to addressing these?

The first key question being:

Is there evidence of an absolute focus on both urgent and important priorities?

The ability of a trust to address both urgent and important issues can often be relatively easy to determine without even stepping foot over the threshold of the organisation.

Undertaking a desk top review of a range of easily available documents can enable an assessment to be quickly made. It is unlikely that any of the relevant documents to support such a review won't be readily available in the public domain. Triangulating recent CQC inspection reports, with information available via a trust's web site and publicly available board papers which should include detail improvement plans, operational performance reports, risk registers, audit reports, strategic objectives and committee minutes/reports, will offer a broad and contemporary foundation upon which to base an assessment of the attention and priority being given by an organisation to those issues recognised as both urgent and important. Having the remit to extensively undertake a review of documentation as an external party may be viewed as a luxury to existing staff unable to carve out the necessary time from daily responsibilities and operational requirements. However, such an exercise should be considered as an achievable and valuable 'stock take' available to all whatever their role. Frequently, the undertaking of such a desk top review identifies aspects that have been overlooked or failed to be given sufficient significance; a case of individuals with challenging portfolios on occasion not being able to see the wood for the trees. Desktop reviews are an amazingly simple activity that does not need to take significant time, can usefully be undertaken by individuals offering a widely differing range of experience or knowledge and yet potentially offer some very helpful insights to inform the development of existing arrangements. Generally, I have found that organisations don't ask enough for desktop reviews of available documentation to be undertaken – this being such a simple way of taking stock and introducing some structured reflection within a challenging fast-paced environment.

The most powerful detailed evidence of priorities being addressed may usually be found within a comprehensive trust wide 'Improvement Plan'. However, one can often find multiple improvement plans to be in place, representing improvement priorities at multiple levels throughout the organisation – departmental, specialty, divisional, site specific etc. This approach presented a challenge to identifying the most urgent issues or the relevant importance of issues across differing plans and the extent to which both the urgent and important issues are being gripped and addressed at pace.

The second key question being:

Is there evidence of effective engagement and understanding of improvement priorities?

The culture of an organisation demonstrated by the leaders that engage with all staff across the organisation to share their vision and values, amongst which is a commitment to quality and ongoing improvement, is key to developing focus and pace for improvements in addition to sustaining those improvements. An explicit organisational approach to improvement, whatever this may be, has been recognised as key to delivering high quality services. An example of this being the effective implementation of the Listening into Action (LIA) project to engage all front-line staff directly in improvement work, which underpinned both the progress of the University Hospitals of Morecambe Bay NHS trust from special measures in 2014 to a trust wide regulatory rating of

Good in 2017 and similarly the progress of Wexham Park NHS Foundation Trust from a trust wide regulatory rating of Inadequate in 2014 to Good in 2016.The CQC published a report in 2017 of case studies from eight NHS trusts which evidenced the importance of effective engagement and communication between leaders and staff[5]. Any such approach, which makes consistent use of a recognised improvement methodology which is seen as a way for the organisation to learn and empowers staff to lead and deliver change, which is supported clearly by the trust board and evident from the ward to board and from outpatients to critical care, should be embedded to evidence grip, pace and sustainability of improvements.

The third key question being:

Is there an explicit recognition and a commitment to addressing the systemic causes of variation?

The NHS is very familiar with the mnemonic acronym S.M.A.R.T. used in highlighting the importance of improvement plan goals and objectives being Specific, Measurable, Achievable, Realistic and Timely to ensure a better chance of accomplishment. The last few years have provided multiple examples of where such SMART action plans have been developed, approved and delivered only for a regulatory inspection to find multiple examples of ongoing concern, presenting evidence of failure to fully address the issues reported as addressed by the action plan. Again, and again this pattern creates a source of confusion, sometimes disbelief and usually profound disappointment that can prove to be demotivating to all involved within the wider system seeking to improve services. In my experience of working with multiple trusts that have experienced this, without fail the reason for this outcome is always directly linked to the trusts failure to focus beyond the symptomatic issues of concern, to identify within their action plan/s the systemic causes for the variation. Trust action/improvement plans that focus only on the specific symptomatic concerns identified or reported to the trust and/or that rely upon a simple Red, Amber, Green (RAG) rating to evaluate and report progress, will lack both the granularity and definition to provide assurance at an operational level. Such plans offer at best evidence of activities undertaken, providing reassurance of efforts being taken. The best of these plans have the potential to offer assurance that an issue has been addressed in a certain department, but not for example to provide assurance that this issue could not reoccur elsewhere. This failure to address the systemic cause of the issue in the first place explaining why a regulator can for example repeatedly report deficiencies in the overcrowding of multiple differing clinic waiting areas, due to the action identified by the trust to address the specific concern being the annual purchase of additional chairs. This action seeking to address the symptom of the overcrowding problem rather than the cause of the problem which rather than pertaining to insufficient chairs was related to poor patient flow. The cause of the issue of poor patient flow requiring in this example for the modification of the criteria used by the booking system to block book appointments to ease the flow of patients through all clinic areas and the subsequent reduction of overcrowding.

Identifying the systemic causes for all undesirable variation allows the essential differentiation of whether an issue of concern is for example a consequence of competing priorities effecting operational capacity, or a more systemic cultural issue possibly indicating capability constraints. Similarly, a variation considered initially to be due to limitations of resource may in fact be caused by deficiencies in operational systems and processes. This differentiation being essential for to identification of the correct actions required to address the issue of concern and to identify the information that will be sought to evidence achievement of the outcomes sought. The importance of explicitly recognising the systemic causes of variation in service provision presenting the most fundamental of principles upon which authentic and sustainable improvements in services can be successfully based upon.

For this essential differentiation to be recognised, a SMART action plan must be SMART 'plus', with the 'plus' representing the additional identification where appropriate of ALL systemic causes of variation recognised within the plan, these explicitly documented and the corresponding evidence of the achievement of desired outcomes, measured as being sustained over time. A simple three level RAG rating system will be found to be insufficient to be used effectively to evaluate a SMART 'plus' improvement plan. A more effective and more granular seven stepped process for evaluating progress and providing assurance of delivery of a SMART 'plus' action/improvement plan being described in greater detail later.

The fourth and final key question being:

Is there a compelling strategic narrative that describes a path to success?

An organisational strategic plan over 5–10 years, accompanied with several relevant enabling strategies that may focus on such areas as workforce, technology and estates, can now be found in most trusts. This strategic clarity is essential to inform and frame decision making at every level within the organisation. In the event that such a compelling narrative can be found, it is essential that this also explicitly informs the organisations approach to driving improvement. By this, I mean that the strategic narrative must be used consistently to assess the significance of any undesirable variations identified. In practice, this requiring the significance of any risk to addressing variation to be evaluated in term of the impact this risk presents to the delivery of strategic objectives. To explain, in simple terms if an identified variation in service delivery is evaluated as not essential to the delivery of the organisation's strategic objectives, then the management action required to address this variation should be considered a low priority. If, however the identified variation in service delivery is evaluated as directly impacting upon the delivery of the organisation's strategic objectives then the management action required to address this variation should be considered of the highest priority. The practicalities of assessing and reporting on this significance will be explored further later as the distinction between the significance of variation as it relates to strategic objectives will be shown to be essential to underpin grip momentum and the sustainability of organisation wide improvements.

Acknowledging that the explanations provided above for each key question focus upon an organisational perspective, I hope that the translation of these questions towards assessing the potential for a given specialist team or location of services, may be easily considered as achievable if this is the specific perspective being sought by the reader. The focus being able to be easily shifted from the organisation wide perspective towards a more defined specific focus by exploring the clarity of specialty business plans, explicitly documented team philosophies of care, locally generated improvement plans and the extent to which staff are actively engaged in transparent clinical governance arrangements. These simple four questions present a framework that can be used by any individual to assess the potential for improvement to be achieved clinically at the bedside or strategically by the board.

Chapter Summary

There are four key questions that can be used to begin to determine an organisation's potential to improve services. This requiring a firm grip of initiatives underway, the necessary pace and momentum of work to address issues and evidence of sustained improvement over time.

The four questions seek evidence of:

1. An absolute focus on both urgent and important priorities.
2. Effective engagement and understanding of improvement priorities.
3. Explicit recognition and a commitment to addressing the systemic causes of variation.
4. A compelling strategic narrative that describes a path to success.

The undertaking of a simple desk top review of publicly available documents offers a simple way for an organisation to take stock, introduce some structured reflection within a challenging fast paced environment and begin to triangulate readily available information to offer a foundation upon which to base an assessment of the organisations potential to improve. These simple questions equally offer the potential for individuals to seek to assess the extent to which a defined area within a trust such as a specific specialist team or services from a given location also have the potential to improve and sustain those improvements.

Chapter 5
An Effective Framework for Assuring Improvement

The term 'assurance' is now a very familiar one that is used daily within every part of every organisation across the NHS. However, despite being so commonly used, it can on occasion be open to interpretation, unhelpfully meaning differing things to differing people. The simple purpose of assurance is to determine if that which is believed to be taking place is indeed happening in practice.

In 2012, the HM Treasury first published some guidance on Assurance Frameworks[6], which detailed how boards of public sector organisations could meet their corporate governance obligations particularly with respect to the delivery of improved, cost effective, public services. Within this guidance assurance is described in the straightforward terms as being an objective examination of evidence for the purpose of providing an independent assessment on governance, risk management and control processes for an organisation.

Additionally, this guidance defines an assurance framework as:

'An Assurance Framework is a structured means of identifying the main sources of assurance in an organisation and coordinating them to best effect.'

How do trust boards assure themselves of progress?

Considerable guidance has subsequently been developed to support trust boards establish board assurance frameworks (BAF) that seek to bring together all relevant information on all the identified all current and future risks facing a trust in achieving its strategic objectives and determining the nature, level and extent of the assurance they will be seeking. NHS Providers in partnership with Baker Tilly have also produced a detailed Board Assurance tool kit for health sector organisations[7] which has been effectively used by multiple organisations to support local consideration regarding the design and application of board assurance arrangements. This tool kit promotes the development of an assurance 'radar' to record the controls in pace to mitigate identified risks relating to core operational activities. The suggested core operational activities identified at this time as relating to strategy, people, estates, information, finance, equipment, and quality and patient experience. Whilst one couldn't argue that these eight suggested operational activities are not fundamental to the achievement of all trust objectives, one might suggest that as the environment within which trusts are operating have increased in complexity over recent years, the ability for all trusts to continually improve services and sustain those improvements has become more challenging due to increasing risks and therefore the necessity for trusts to identify strong and consistent controls to optimise improvement has increased in importance. It is however reasonably rare to find a trust that explicitly identifies these issues within its BAF. The recognition and establishment of explicit controls that are tailor made to directly relate to providing assurance on the organisations ability to improve services will provide a framework to produce good quality management information that will in turn generate robust evidence that offers certainty and confidence that what needs to be happening locally is actually happening in practice.

How can you assess an organisation's ability to drive improvement?

As a precursor to exploring what maybe best practice in term of improving services, we need to clarify the context within which all forthcoming information relates by identifying the primary controls that will provide assurance of improvement and complete the introduction of all the elements required to be present within an effective assurance framework that focuses explicitly upon an organisation's ability to improve. Two of these elements we have already touched upon. These relating to:

1. A **SMART 'plus' action/improvement plan** that recognises the systemic causes of variation responsible for the cause-and-effect reaction that has resulted in the symptomatic issues of concern. For such a plan to be SMART 'plus', we have already identified that the 'plus' needs to represent the additional identification where appropriate of ALL systemic causes of variation within the plan, requiring these to be explicitly documented together with the corresponding evidence of the achievement

of desired outcomes, measured as being sustained over time. A SMART 'plus' action plan providing a strong evidential base that will support a focused approach being sustained to address the recognised and agreed systemic causes of variation. This approach being able to withstand any unhelpful, inappropriate or ill-advised internal or external pressure or influence to alter the documented focus of improvements.

2. The use of a **seven stepped process for evaluating progress** that provides operational assurance of delivery of an improvement plan. Again, we have already identified that this approach is predicated on the acceptance that a simple three level RAG rating system will be found to be insufficient to be used effectively to evaluate the progress and delivery of a SMART 'plus' improvement plan. A simple 3 level RAG rating being unable to summarise an evaluation of progress that should reflect three fundamental aspects of performance, that ideally need to be jointly assessed for a fair evaluation of progress to be undertaken. These fundamental aspects to include an evaluation of the impact of initiatives undertaken on the symptom of the issue, an assessment of the effectiveness of initiatives undertaken to address the systemic reason for that symptom and an explicit evaluation of the desired outcome achieved over an agreed period.

The remaining three elements not yet explicitly introduced relate to:

3. The importance of **developing an effective degree of internal independence.** Proactively strengthening the degree of internal independence serves to safeguard against potential aspects of advocacy and self-interest which have the potential of significantly effecting internal rigour and objectivity. The absence of internal independence in the evaluation of the delivery of improvement initiatives poses a significant risk to the degree of independence present within a process of developing and delivering any type of organisational improvement plan. Recognising and exploring the very prevalent risks posed by advocacy and self-interest and the perfect storm that can be created if selective blindness also features in this mix, begins to develop an understanding of the detrimental impact an absence of internal independence can have on rigour and objectivity when developing and evaluating the effectiveness of local improvement plans. The primary risk of an absence if internal independence being the ease with which reassurance regarding activity being undertaken to deliver an improvement plan is generated as opposed to the required generation of evidence that offers robust assurance in the delivery of the intended outcomes.
4. The importance of developing detailed **definitions of strategic assurance levels** to inform the board of progress. The recommended granular definitions of

effective strategic assurance levels recognise the benefits of seeking to replicate the established standards of best practice available via external auditors to promote consistency of understanding, application and interpretation of strategic assurance levels. In due course we will explore how it will be appropriate for such definitions to explicitly refer to the rationale for each level of assurance. This rationale including reference to the design and effective operation of the existing system (For improvement), the effectiveness of controls in place, the potential impact upon the achievement of the organisation's strategic objectives, the risks to the organisation's reputation or other strategic risks and finally the significance of any managerial action identified as required to be taken. Adopting four clearly defined levels of assurance will significantly reduce the reliance on personal judgements of individuals within the organisation, mitigating the potential risk of selective blindness present at an individual, team or organisational level.

5. The importance of the **assurance subcommittees of the trust board working effectively**. Subcommittees working effectively and interdependently with other committees to provide assurance regarding the implementation of agreed strategies is what is required to influence and inform the decision making of the trust board. With the role of NEDs being to both develop organisational strategy and review the performance of executive directors the opportunity that NED led effective committee working offers for

undertaking scrutiny and objective review of executive performance to provide assurance of the implementation of strategic objectives is considerable. Optimising the information reported to assurance sub-committees through using a seven-stepped process for evaluating delivery of improvement plans, with steps taken to build in internal independence of reporting in addition to adopting best practice strategic definitions of assurance will all contribute significantly to the effectiveness of all committees, their focus and subsequent reporting to the trust board.

Each of these five elements briefly outlined above and represented below should be viewed as of equal importance and will be the focus of a chapter each to explore in detail.

Elements of an Effective Assurance Framework:

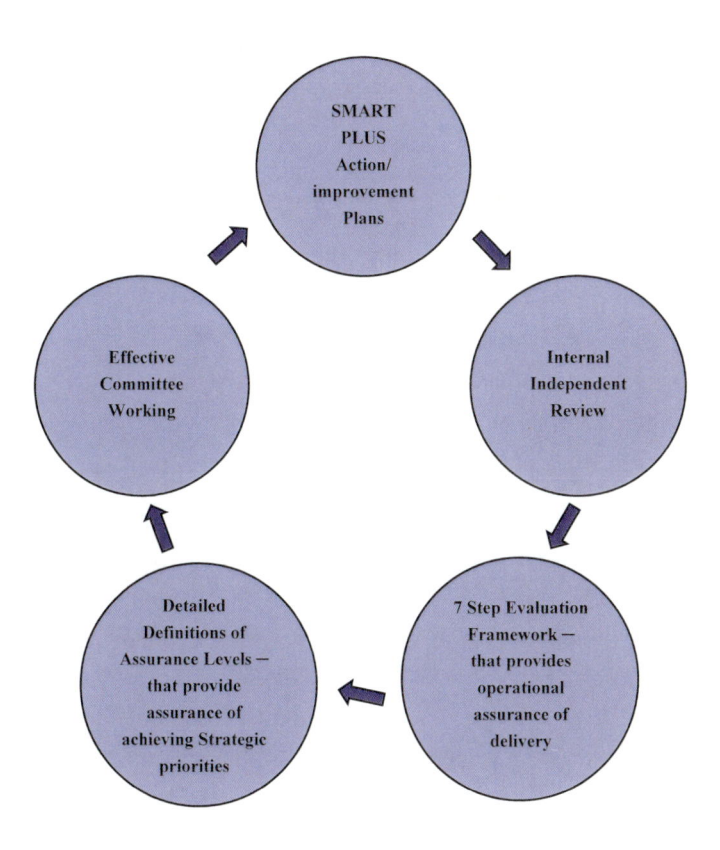

- SMART PLUS Action/improvement Plans
- Internal Independent Review
- 7 Step Evaluation Framework — that provides operational assurance of delivery
- Detailed Definitions of Assurance Levels — that provide assurance of achieving Strategic priorities
- Effective Committee Working

Can these key elements only be applied strategically?

Being mindful that as a reader of this book you might be an experienced executive director, a newly appointed ward sister or hold any number of differing professional roles in between, it is important to recognise that the five key elements of a framework for assuring improvement as described above can effectively be explored and applied by any individual at any level within a trust. The subtitle of this book being 'Improving Services from the Bedside to the Boardroom' is a truth, the successful translation and application of the issues being explored simply requiring some rudimentary interpretation. Viewing the five key elements described above as guiding principles supports the application of a little pragmatic adjustment to reflect either the language used within your own organisation or the operational and governance structures within it. Have confidence that you know your organisation better than anyone and certainly better than me. Seek to explore and interpret the principles outlined above in a way that you believe might have most impact to your local situation. The focus of this book being to share observations, learning and identified best practice from a wide range of trusts and to do so in a way that adds value to those of you in difficult roles, within challenging environments, who possibly consider that there is little time or opportunity to achieve anything other than what is considered from day to day to be both urgent and important. Please do not fall into the trap of believing it either necessary or indeed desirable to seek to replicate everything summarised above. Consider this chapter as outlining the 'menu' for your consideration. As we begin to explore in greater detail each of these elements and as we seek to practically explain and offer options and opportunities for strengthening your approach to improving services, you will begin to identify the pragmatic and achievable choices that you might wish to make from this menu. If there is one obvious aspect of the five outlined key areas that you are struggling with or consider to be your Achilles heel, then I would encourage you to focus there. I have worked with trusts that over considerable time have sought to maintain a single focus on continuing to strengthen their SMART 'plus' action plan with the aim of establishing an increasingly firm foundation for all other aspects of governance process, which has proved to be an extremely effective approach. It's not that they haven't recognised the importance of the other areas within the assurance framework but that they understand the limitations of their capacity for change and have made a conscious decision to maintain a strong focus on one single aspect to embed practice to make this a driver for further change. If you however for example, feel that your existing action plan is sufficiently SMART 'plus' as there is a widespread confidence that it is fit for purpose but you are concerned regarding the lack of internal operational challenge regarding progress reports generated, then you may find you have a greater appetite for understanding the options for developing an increased internal degree of independence in evaluating progress and find yourself focusing on the particular chapter exploring this further to identify your local opportunities for achieving this.

If you are working directly at the bedside, as a specialist auditing defined aspect of care, as a matron responsible for local accreditation processes or as a care group quality lead, you may find it more appropriate to interpret the importance of the effective working of assurance sub-committees as relating to the effectiveness of your local divisional/care group local governance group/committee. The requirements that have been described for effective working being completely translatable in term of the importance of your local divisional/care group committee working interdependently with other existing groups/committees in other divisions/care groups. If however, you are an established member of the corporate team working directly with the trust board, then I would hope the outline of the key elements and principles as they have been described above, are easily able to be translated for consideration within your local arrangements and offer some stimulation to considering how these can be translated and applied for the potential benefit of all levels within and across your organisation.

Chapter Summary

The simplest definition of an Assurance Framework is a structured means of identifying the main sources of assurance in an organisation and coordinating them to best effect. Within this, the recognition and establishment of explicit controls that are tailor made to directly relate to providing assurance on the organisations ability to improve services will generate robust evidence that offers certainty and confidence that what needs to be happening locally is actually happening in practice.

Key five key elements of a framework for Assuring Improvement include:

1. A SMART 'plus' Improvement plan
2. A 7 stepped process for evaluating operational delivery and progress
3. An effective degree of local independence
4. Detailed definitions of Strategic Assurance levels
5. Effective Assurance sub-committee working

All five elements are of equal importance and may be strengthened individually or collectively in response to identified local needs. Focusing on any one area for development will impact positively upon all other areas, strengthen the focus of efforts and build confidence in the judgements reached regarding progress made.

Chapter 6
SMART 'Plus' Action/Improvement Plans

As we have introduced, the existence of a SMART 'plus' action/improvement plan is the most fundamental of the five key elements that I have found in organisations with effective assurance arrangements. The scope of any such plan is therefore critical to its potential to transform services as required or intended. Let's use a painting analogy to explore this further.

Identifying the scope of your improvement plan?

Painting by Numbers → Copying Best Practice → Creating an Original

Painting By Numbers or Producing an Original?

The overarching aim of any improvement plan is to support delivery of the improvement intentions of the organisation. Very early on in my working with trusts across the country, I began to recognise improvement plans as falling into three main categories. The first I would describe as doing painting by numbers. This approach was most prevalent in the initial years of the CQC undertaking comprehensive organisation wide inspections and often referred to in trusts as a 'CQC action plan'. This type of plan simply sought to replicate the issues of concern reported on by the CQC. It often failed to seek significantly to identify the underlying causes of these concerns and in the main described solutions that directly mirror these concerns. For example, the regulator reported the requirement to improve mandatory training levels for nursing staff, with the action plan confirming this action with progress reports pertaining to clarifying mandatory training levels for nursing staff. Such action plans were limited primarily if not solely to addressing the concerns raised by others be the CQC, other professional regulators, or external stakeholders. They did not seek to understand or address the systemic reasons for any concerns raised by others and did not begin to identify improvement priorities deemed a priority by the organisation. A painting by numbers approach as evidenced by a CQC action plan as described above, were not found in high performing organisation as they all without exception did not limit themselves to reactively focusing on addressing issues identified by others. Such a painting by numbers approach has only the potential at best to achieve partial improvements regarding a limited perspective that are most likely to only be sustained for a short period of time. This approach was initially adopted by several struggling trusts in 'special measures'; these trusts all failed to make any significant progress until this approach significantly matured to demonstrate an understanding of the need to address systemic causes of variation to transform services in preference to a focus on symptomatic issues that at best could be described as resulting in short term transactional improvements.

Aspiring to Producing a Copy of a Masterpiece?

The second category that plans fall into; I would describe as one in painting terms that seeks to copy a masterpiece produced by another i.e., replicating best practice from elsewhere. Such a plan is often referred to in trusts as a more generic 'quality action/improvement plan'. There is much that is commendable regarding this approach as it significantly evidences recognition of best practice achieved elsewhere, together with an openness to learn and adopt such practice locally. Such plans therefore seek to not only address concerns raised by others be this the CQC, other professional regulators, or external stakeholders but also commendably evidence the intention to learn from others to address issues prioritised for development that support the delivery of the organisation's strategic objectives. As we have explored, a high performing organisation is interested in what other organisations are doing well and how they are achieving this. Reassuringly, most trust improvement plans seem now to fall into this category. Lessons have been learned by those trust stuck deep in the special measures trench for some years, although caution should be recommended, as simply replicating initiatives successful in addressing issues in other trusts will only have the same effect if the organisations share the same systemic reasons for the issues arising in the first place. A local approach to identifying these systemic root causes being essential in addition to having an openness to adopt best practice from elsewhere.

Aiming to Create Something Original and Authentic?

The third and final category of plans can be described in painting terms as equivalent to developing an original masterpiece, seeking to produce an original piece of work that only makes complete sense for the organisation it relates to. These plans powerfully convey the intentions of the organisation and address the systemic causes of concerns raised internally or externally. They recognise and prioritise the translation of best practice from other trusts recognised as outstanding in a given field, in addition to including those improvements prioritised as required by the trust because of its own audit and review processes. These plans commit to a deep and forensic programme of improvements considering innovative solutions not yet tried and tested elsewhere with the aim of achieving the strategic aims and objectives agreed by the organisation. In reading such a plan, you are left in no doubt as to the priorities of the organisation and how these priorities are going to be met. Such plans are often appropriately referred to as trust wide improvement plans; providing the bedrock for grip, pace and sustainability of improvements directed towards delivering strategic objectives. Some powerful examples of such plans are now reassuringly evident in an increasing number of trusts. These trusts are recognised as high performing and display many of the characteristics explored earlier. The effectiveness of these plans needs to inform recognised best practice across the NHS. The NHS is in trouble and the establishment of organisational improvement plans that meet the standards described above are urgently needed to educate and inform stakeholders regarding the systemic root causes of current challenges with a given trust's performance. The potential impact that such plans could have in effectively calling out and overcoming the endemic external selective blindness that currently exists is required to optimise both the performance of each individual trust and the NHS as a whole.

The Limitations of Historical Plans:

As we have begun to explore, if one accepts that an explicit recognition and commitment to addressing the systemic causes of variation is an essential characteristic of a trust that has the potential to improve services and sustain improvement over time, one must also accept that a SMART 'plus' action plan that recognises and seeks to address the root cause of any variation will be required to drive all improvement activities. This drive established through the recording all systemic causes of variation recognised and all the necessary evidence of delivery of the action plan and the oversight arrangements in place to evaluate the achievement of desired outcomes.

Historically, many SMART action/improvement plans developed within the NHS and presented in a variety of differing ways have not achieved this, being limited to broadly capturing the following elements:

- A Reference to the Source of the Concern
- The Location/Division/Specialty in question
- The Issue of Concern
- Action/s to directly address the identified concern
- An Executive Lead/Action Owner
- Start/Completion dates
- Summary of Progress
- Red, Amber, Green (RAG) rating of delivery

The presentation of such action plans has undoubtedly developed over recent years alongside the recognition that the development of a central/corporate resource is also beneficial to support the ongoing development, updating and reporting upon the delivery of the action plan. This central/corporate resource often being in the form of a programme management office provided much needed capacity to support divisional progress made to deliver the identified improvements. However, as already highlighted, despite such clear commitments being made by some trusts to address identified concerns, this approach has repeatedly been shown following a regulatory inspection or serious incidents taking place, to not necessarily be effective in addressing the root cause of the initial issue/concern raised. All too often a cycle is then established of developing a much more detailed action plan, utilising the same template; in addition to providing additional central resource to evidence greater emphasis being placed on the development and delivery of the action plan. Of course, focusing more resource and effort to the same approach not unsurprisingly yields the same results. One such trust that I was initially invited to work with that had been in special measures for some time, had reached a position where they had 77 separate action plans in place! It took the appointment of a new Executive Director of Nursing with responsibility to lead quality to take stock of this situation and realise that continuing with this approach would continue to yield the same results. With the support of a newly appointed CEO, she sought some fresh independent eyes to help in reviewing the approach being taken by the organisation. I designed and delivered a workshop for the senior leadership team where informed by a detailed desk top review of available documentation, and some reflections regarding the lack of progress, progress was soon made in beginning to articulate the first improvement plan for the organisation that not only began to recognise the systemic causes of the many long standing issues but also began to prioritise alongside this what it locally wished to improve and what the organisational approach to improvement would be to begin to develop a wide body of staff who would not only know what good looked like but also would be ambassadors across the organisation supporting the service transformation that was being sought. This workshop was a very small but critical action: the first of many that enabled this organisation to steadily and consistently develop a single SMART 'plus' improvement plan that laid a path for this trust to incrementally improve, sustain this improvement and in due course exit the special measures regime.

The Potential of a SMART 'Plus' plan:

So, what are the important additional elements required for a SMART action plan to be SMART 'plus'? The key difference being that during the process of developing the action plan forensic attention is given to identifying those organisational aspects of selective blindness that if left unaddressed will prevent sustainable improvement being achieved. In addition to the basic elements already identified in a SMART plan, the additional elements required to ensure the plan is SMART 'plus' and all systemic causes of variation are addressed, and evidence of delivery evaluated consistently are:

- The underlying root cause of the identified concern.
- Explicit outcomes sought.
- The information available and required to evidence delivery.
- The specific committee providing oversight of the work.
- Rating delivery against seven operational assurance levels.

Many existing SMART action plans in use to good effect have developed to include some or parts of these elements. To establish the consistency required to drive improvements that are focused, at pace and most importantly sustainable, all the four additional elements need to be developed to be a part of every aspect of a trust's SMART 'plus' improvement plan. I'm sure it will not go unnoticed to the reader that these additional elements begin to reinforce the interdependency between all the five characteristics of a strong assurance framework introduced in the previous chapter. The significance of reflecting these elements within a SMART 'plus' action plan being to establish a bedrock to support and reinforce the importance of these characteristics for each improvement initiative identified as required.

Challenges Posed by Administration:

I have been invited to review numerous trust improvement plans to offer an independent view of delivery. Whilst this in itself is a very positive action for a trust to take, which demonstrates a commendable commitment to self-evaluation and improvement, it has proved often to identify some significant weaknesses in current arrangement which can be of great surprise and generate a fair degree of discomfort. Fortunately, if an organisation has taken the decision to open itself to an independent review it usually means that the senior leaders within it are sufficiently robust to whether a little discomfort for the benefit of identifying some opportunities for strengthening existing arrangements and further improving services to become recognised as high quality. An athlete might offer that there can be no gain without some pain!

In commencing such reviews, I have often found multiple versions of an action plan in use simultaneously across differing divisions in a trust, often with an equal number of administrative errors due to overly complex internal arrangements in place involving multiple individuals across the organisation contributing to updating these plans. Staff are often balancing many differing priorities and whilst the establishment of a corporate resource to support the administration of an improvement plan can be hugely appreciated by clinical teams focused upon delivering the changes required, a central control of administrative processes can also create delays to updating plans and confusion as to what constitutes the most up to date version if an easily accessible communication platform is not utilised to ensure that everyone directly involved in the development and delivery of an improvement plan has the ability to update the plan in real time and have immediate access to the latest version at any time. The trust in special measures with multiple improvement plans which indicated a commendable intention to improve services could not in any way hope to accurately update or effectively monitor these without significant capacity and capability being redirected from operational service delivery, which would have been in direct opposition to that which was strategically was aiming to be achieved. The considerable time this trust spent on engaging staff to develop a single plan as described earlier, presented a solid foundation for clearly defined processes for updating and circulating the plan that ensured the development of familiarisation with the agreed priorities and a consistent understanding of the latest performance position.

What Is Required for the Development of a Robust Plan?

There are some very talented and enthusiastic individuals now working in a range of relatively new quality improvement roles that have been established with the aim of supporting clinical teams in developing, updating and reporting on the delivery of planned improvements. In small trusts that I work with, these roles may be confined to part time positions within defined divisions or clinical teams. In larger organisations such roles may also be supplemented by a small corporate team providing a routine bridge of communication between clinical teams and executive leads.

All arrangements need to appropriately reflect the size of the organisation to be cost effective. Some of the most effective arrangements I have come across have been established within some of the largest trusts in the country operating under a group model. Here I have experienced clearly defined differing layers of colleagues focused wholly upon supporting the development and delivery of improvement action plans which additionally also present a clearly defined opportunity for building in independence of evaluation. Developing a robust level of internal independence is another of the critical elements always found within effective assurance arrangements, which we will focus on in detail later.

The Case for Less Haste More Speed:

There is often considerable pressure exerted upon an organisation following a regulatory inspection or external audit of any nature to develop an action plan swiftly to demonstrate the existence of corporate capacity, capability and commitment to address any externally identified concerns as speedily as possible. Against this pressure it is completely understandable that short cuts might be taken to provide reassurance to external parties of the ability of the senior leadership team is up to the job. This can often result in some common mistakes being made. A generic example being a trust receives regulatory feedback that there appeared to not be a policy for the handling of a specific issue. It is immaterial what the issue is, it could relate to communicating triage waiting times or disinfecting side rooms. The trust seeks to immediately acknowledge this concern in an action plan, confirming that a long-standing policy in place for the issue in question. The policy is then referenced in the action plan, with the RAG rating recorded as green and at the earliest available opportunity the specific action is closed as completed. In this scenario, non-executive directors can be very reassured as can external parties that such swift clarity has been provided on seemingly removing this issue as a concern. I have found this to be a very common response, which only serves to create unfounded reassurance that the required policies are all in place until the next regulatory inspection is undertaken and feedback is received whereby concerns are repeated or possibly described using different language or a changed perspective. This lack of improvement possibly stimulating a degree of challenge or disbelief, further actions committed to and undertaken in anticipation of another inspection. So, let's explore this example further, using the reference of an absent policy for disinfecting side rooms. If at the point of recording in the action plan the specific concern regarding the absence of a policy to disinfect side rooms was subjected to even a rudimentary root-cause-analysis to identify the systemic cause of this concern the following might have been identified. To the potential question why staff interviewed were unaware of the trust's policy on disinfecting side rooms, the response may have been very clear that the specific staff asked about this were all domestic agency staff who had not received an adequate induction and therefore, unaware of the comprehensive policy in place. The required action to address the root cause of this initially identified concern needing therefore to be related to the process of inducting temporary staff; a very different action to be reflected in the action plan in order to address the original issue but one which has the potential of establishing a sustainable improvement of the symptomatic concern raised. With the reasonable expectation that with assurance available to evidence that improvements to the cause of the issue, the induction process had been made, the symptomatic concern regarding the disinfection of side rooms should not be raised again.

Alternatively, to the potential question why staff interviewed were unaware of the trust's policy on disinfecting side rooms, the response may have been very clear that the specific staff asked about this were all senior nursing staff who were well aware and familiar with the trust's detailed disinfection policy. This rudimentary root-cause-analysis (RCA) identifying that senior nursing staff had repeatedly escalated concerns to senior manager regarding potential gaps within this policy, seeking additional detail to be provided within the policy to strengthen requirements regarding the disinfection of side rooms. This root cause requiring action to potentially address both why concerns escalated by senior nursing staff had not been acted upon in a timely way and the policy revision to clarify side room disinfection requirements. The identification of the underlying cause of the identified concern being essential in the development of a SMART 'plus' action plan to generate grip, pace and sustainability of improvements.

The Necessity for Distinguishing Between Observations, Experiences and Root Causes:

The simple examples outlined above demonstrate the significance of undertaking even the most basic of root cause analysis in order to explore the reason for the variation identified, rather than accepting the issue in question at face value. The regulator will be largely highlighting observations and experiences. It is for the organisation to explore why these occurred. Addressing the initially reported concern may present a straightforward opportunity to demonstrate an organisation may be able to generate pace and momentum towards improvement but it is very unlikely that over time the organisation will be able to sustain this improvement due to the symptom rather than the cause being the focus of improvement activity. Given the absolute necessity to identify the systemic root causes of any variation to address successfully and sustainably any symptomatic issues of concern identified within an organisation, we shall look separately at this is greater detail.

How to Strengthen Reporting of Progress?

In ensuring the use of RAC to develop the content of a SMART 'plus' improvement plan, the process of gathering evidence to provide assurance of delivery is an important aspect of any coordinated approach to updating the plan and generating reports of progress. This is without doubt the aspect where I have found there often to be most confusion and inconsistency within trusts. This almost always related to the absence of a sufficient focus on the systemic cause of the variation in question, where the generation of information on progress has focused upon the status of the symptom rather than evidencing the addressing of the root cause of the issue.

The most comprehensive of action plans that I have reviewed, refer to available information or reports identified as key to evidencing delivery of the initiatives in train and achievement of the outcomes being sought. This effectively signposting the reader to evidence which in turn will require a degree of independent review to confirm. The practicalities of this we will pick up in a future chapter when exploring the importance of developing internal independence as a key element of effective assurance arrangements.

The format of the improvement plan influences the ease by which a single comprehensive plan may potentially be updated by several colleagues at different times and how quickly reports may be generated for different purposes and audiences. The use of an excel spreadsheet rather than a word document offering a range of efficient options for filtering content to aid evaluation of overall progress being made.

The skills acquired to support remote working during the Covid-19 pandemic, has included widespread familiarity of utilising Microsoft Teams. The use of this communication platform which is now routine practice across the NHS, offers an unparalleled opportunity for the time efficient connection and contribution from a disparate number of colleagues responsible for updating the plan on a regular basis, usually weekly. The full use of the functions available via this platform for undertaking online meetings (Calling or video), screen sharing to support understanding, recording facilities to provide reinforcement, file sharing to promote inclusivity and the ability to store and share files in real time, provides a time efficient solution to the provision of updates, revisions and evaluations from a range of contributors virtually simultaneously. In all the trusts I have worked with during the pandemic, whilst there has been distinct improvement made in connecting and engaging with colleagues through virtual means, I have come across only one trust where the full potential of utilising the Microsoft Teams platform was near to being realised. The unusual IT background that the Director of Operations came from in this trust was given widespread acknowledgement across the organisation of this being the reason for these positive and much appreciated arrangements, which respected the most valuable commodity of people's time and significantly reduced historical routine administrative errors. There is generally a great deal that could be improved upon regarding the efficiency and effectiveness of the way trusts routinely engage and communicate with colleagues regarding a complex portfolio of work such an organisational wide improvement plan. My experience of working on similar portfolios of work with the private sector has been the opposite, with the potential of Microsoft Teams fully utilised, and skills quickly transferred to colleagues less familiar with the platform to ensure optimum use of individuals' availability, time and expertise, which in turn increases the effectiveness of everyone involved in delivering the specific project. So often in the NHS we do well at getting the best people into difficult roles but fail to get the best out of them. If you feel this may apply to you, consider carefully how the systems and processes underpinning the ongoing development of your local improvement plan could be adjusted to improve the effectiveness of all colleagues contributing to this work. An impactful SMART 'plus' improvement plan will require the effective collaborative working of a range of disparate colleagues with work plans probably impossible to coordinate. Full utilisation of a communication platform such as Microsoft Teams optimises the available valuable expertise and will ensure professional administration and availability of all relevant documents, including robust version control arrangements.

Chapter 7
Root-Cause-Analysis (RCA)

How Is Root-cause Analysis Used Effectively Across the NHS?

It is interesting given the widespread use within the NHS of using root-cause-analysis to investigate complaints and serious incidents, why this valuable approach has not become routine practice within quality improvement activities in trusts. Possibly, as much of the requirements for improvements can come from external stakeholders; be these regulators, commissioners, strategists or politicians, where attention may be focused on specific symptomatic failings, the drive to address these symptomatic issues in a timely way diverts from the more measured approach of bringing together differing perspectives on an issue to identify the root cause. This possibility is of course based on the assumption that the root cause of the issue which may or may not be known by the external stakeholder is also NOT known by the trust. In this scenario, where a specific issue of concern is raised by an external party for which there is no appreciation of the root cause, the undertaking and documentation of a RCA following a process which invites the external stakeholder to be actively involved will be the most effective approach to agreeing actions to be taken and the priority to be given to these. For example, in the event of a commissioner raising a concern regarding the trust's response times for handling a specific patient's complaint, a response to this symptomatic issue might include greater priority being given to concluding this process with oversight from the relevant director. On face value such action is likely to be welcomed by the complainant and potentially demonstrate the responsiveness of the trust in addressing issues of concern, providing a seemingly swift resolution to the issue. This issue can though only not reoccur if the cause of this issue was directly related to reduced capacity at a point in time to meet response timescales. If, however a RCA was undertaken to identify the cause that ultimately affected this delayed handling of this complaint, it may have been identified that the cause was more significant and relating to a fundamental lack of clarity regarding systems and process for investigating complaints. This identified root cause necessitating the agreement of a range of actions having wider impact across the organisation in order to generate confidence that such concerns have been addressed to improve this aspect of performance in the longer term. The outcome of taking this approach being not only limited to achieving sustainable improvements but in many cases, educating the stakeholder regarding the complexity of an issue and the need to focus on improving the systemic drivers of performance rather that improving symptomatic aspects of that performance. Consistently taking this approach more importantly effectively identified the systemic drivers, the root causes of issues effecting a trust's performance that are both within the trusts' direct ability to influence and improve and essentially those which lie outside of the trust's direct sphere of influence. The example above of handling complaints in a timely way, having both potential symptomatic and systemic causes for the issue that are directly within the trust's sphere of influence and therefore reasonable for the stakeholder to set expectations for improvement and hold individuals to account for delivering these improvements.

Why are Root-causes of Variation Not Routinely Captured in Improvement Plans?

In my experience, the root causes of performance issues identified by a trust within a trust are often widely known, and the root cause often identified at the outset as the issue of concern. This is ideal and should result in the identification of a number of initiatives that will have the desired impact of both addressing symptomatic concerns, identified contributing factors and most importantly, the identified root cause, to ensure the sustainability of required improvements. However, equally often one can find the specific relationship of cause and effect to be not explicitly recognised or documented, possibly because the root cause is not understood, has been overlooked in favour of more easily identified contributory factors, misconstrued, considered too difficult or viewed as impossible to address. This is precisely the scenario where the root cause is essential to be identified, recognised by all stakeholders and a collaborative approach to identifying an improvement plan to address these systemic causes of undesired variation agreed upon. The importance of this requiring us to explore further a little later.

What Exactly Is a Root-cause?

The root cause is the core issue that sets in motion a cause and effect reaction that ultimately leads to the problem or identified concern. An RCA can involve a wide variety of tools and techniques, the use of fishbone diagrams, risk tree diagrams, barrier analysis etc. A quick Google search is all that is needed to inform and provide easy to apply techniques that can be used. There are multiple sites that offer easy to access guidance on a wide range of problem-solving approaches to 'Quality Management'. These techniques all offer a framework for systematically identifying and considering all the potential contributing and root causes for an issue of concern; causes potentially pertaining to policy frameworks, systems processes and procedures, people, equipment, environment and supplies. Using these recognised techniques to explore all the potential causes and collecting and analysing data to prioritise these will enable the identification of all the contributing causes in addition to the specific root cause; with this simple and straightforward approach documented. The fundamental basis of a RCA simply requires the question 'why is this happening' to be asked of the defined problem or issue. For each response, the question 'why is that' must continue to be posed until all contributing causes have been recognised and the highest-level cause of the initial problem is confirmed, representing the root cause of the issue. Asking 'why' five times is felt to usually be sufficient to uncover the root cause of the problem in question. Addressing this identified root cause providing the opportunity for sustainable improvement of the symptomatic identified issues of concern.

The Risks and Limitations of Undertaking a RCA Singlehandedly:

So given that there is evidence that the knowledge and experience to undertake root-cause analysis is in place and being utilised across the NHS for other purposes, one might for the purpose of demonstration be tempted to test out this approach on the issue of concern to identify why RCA is not used in a routine way for the purposes of developing improvement plans. For the purposes of such a demonstration, I thought I should have a go.

Problem:	Root-cause analysis is not routinely used by trusts to develop action plans to sustain improvements.
Why?	The timescale within which an agreed action plan is required by the trust to be produced does not allow root cause analysis to be undertaken.
Why?	External stakeholders require immediate evidence of priority being given by the executive team towards addressing identified issues. This to be provided in the form of a comprehensive agreed action plan being actively progressed.
Why?	Key individuals potentially demonstrate selective blindness regarding the significance of the initial variations identified, accepting these as the issues requiring immediate attention.
Why?	The root causes of the issues identified could potentially relate to wickedly challenging issues that would require multi-faceted solutions beyond the direct influence of the trust.
Why?	The solutions potentially required to address potential root causes are considered unachievable given constraints of resources and current external stakeholders' appetite.

Whilst some readers might be of the view that the above analysis is fair, the fact that I have undertaken this analysis alone creates risks to the validity of its conclusion. As has been acknowledged, all of us have the potential to display unintended bias and must be vigilant regarding our own selective blindness regarding issues. We must remember that selective blindness can present in us all – reflecting the limitations of our experience and gaps in our specialist knowledge. We will all have bias and prejudices that can distort our perception of issues and contribute to blind spots. No one is exempt from having blind spots. Due to this RCA is most effectively undertaken in a small group, with participants offering differing perspectives and knowledge of the situation being examined. Such a group is likely to be readily formed within an organisation in the throes of developing or revising an improvement plan. The benefits of inviting representatives of key stakeholders are obvious in terms of building a consensus for initiatives to be taken through increased understanding of the interdependencies of issues. Integrating the use of RCA to refine and update an improvement plan also ensures the plan remains dynamic and responsive to new information that may come to light because of ongoing analysis and the use of some of the many specific tools and techniques that might be warranted in certain circumstances. Consistently using RCA will also ensure that potential influence of individual selective blindness is limited and is unable to grow and take hold across an organisation, contributing to a culture of continuous improvement.

The Benefits of Undertaking a RCA Collectively:

A SMART 'plus' action plan that identifies both the concerns initially identified and the root causes of those concerns will ensure that the systemic causes on any past variation will become the focus of improvement initiatives to be addressed in a sustainable way to reduce variation going forward. To achieve this it is essential that the correct root cause is identified by a group with differing perspectives to ensure that any improvement achieved are sustainable. The table below offers some examples of this:

	Example of a potential concern identified	Potential initial RCA undertaken by an individual	Potential confirmed RCA undertaken by a group
1	Need to improve compliance with safeguarding training	System for recording training not fit for purpose	Established cultural norms present no consequences to non-compliance.
2	Need to improve complaint response times	Long term vacancies in roles responsible for drafting complain responses	Established cultural norms present no consequences to providing late responses.
3	Need to ensure all available equipment is within serviceable dates for use	Not all clinical equipment included in centralise servicing arrangements	Established cultural norms present no consequences to not ensuring equipment is serviced.
4	Need to ensure all mental capacity act assessments	Budgeted staffing levels for some clinical	Established cultural norms present no

| | documentation is completed in full | areas have directly impacted upon the capacity available to undertake full assessments. | consequences to non-compliance. |

The four examples of potential concerns given above relating to compliance with safeguarding training, complaint response times, use of serviceable equipment and mental capacity act documentation may appear at face value to not be connected. They may initially be considered by individuals demonstrating their own degree of selective blindness, to be unfortunate slips in standards that are confined to specific clinical areas or teams that will be addressed through focused initiatives directed towards those areas. A commendable approach and an initial attempt by a single individual to identify the underlying cause of these four seemingly unconnected issues if carried out without discussion, exploration and challenge, may offer a range of reasons for these variations, as outlined above. It is likely that individuals attempting to undertake RCA alone will identify relevant contributory factors that may prove helpful to address but unlikely to identify the true root cause of an issue, which will be required to ensure sustainability of any improvement over time. Exploring more closely the first potential concern regarding the need to improve compliance with safeguarding training, might be thought to be the consequence of poor recording on the corporate system used for monitoring compliance, this requiring the identification of a rectifying action of updating the IT system. However, a more effective

RCA undertaken and informed by differing perspectives and knowledge, may move past this initially identified contributory factor, confirming the true root cause as being related to there being no consequences in the organisation for not undertaking or recording the training undertaken; this representing a very different cultural issue requiring very different actions to be taken for this issue of concern to be sustainably addressed.

Similarly, with the other three concerns that relate to complaint response times, the servicing of equipment and documentation, initial underlying causes may be identified by an individual as relating to vacancies, system failures, resources and capacity. Those issues presenting a logical and reasonable rationale for the concerns raised, representing valid contributory factors. Undertaking a more effective RCA might again move past these initial issues/contributory factors to identify the true root causes of all concerns, with these again relating directly to the culture within the organisation of there being little or no consequences to not meeting defined standards of behaviour or practice. Using RCA to find that a range of seemingly disparate initial concerns are associated with the same identified root cause emphasises the organisational significance of addressing the identified root cause. To achieve this clarity and focus takes time, which as we have explored circumstances does not always seem to be made available to leadership teams. There is nothing wrong with identifying an initial root cause which seems to be logical and reasonable, given a timescale set by others, so long as these continue to be refined through wider engagement and when confirmed these reflected within a SMART 'plus' action plan that commits to initiatives and actions to address these agreed root causes. When this occurs one often observes the absolute root causes of multiple symptomatic concerns being able to be distilled to a small number of duplicated root causes. This powerful clarity being potentially transformative for an organisation as it is the route to achieving grip, momentum and sustainability of improvements.

The Importance of Realising That the Same Problem Can Be a Result of Differing Causes:

If one reviews several CQC inspection reports from differing organisations one cannot fail but to begin to recognise some systemic strategic causes of variation affecting the quality of services provided across the NHS. Obvious examples of these reoccurring systemic causes of variation relating to the recruitment and retention of staff, or the provision of services from buildings no longer fit for purpose. Comparing reports can also identify some seemingly 'small' local issues that appear to affect a significant number of organisations and ones that indicate a concern for standards within the most discrete of areas. There is one example which seems to have regularly featured in reports of trusts of all sizes and specialisms...*fridge temperatures!* Not only can fridge temperatures be a very reliable indicator of the consistency of standards maintained within a team but it is also a good simple example of the importance of identifying the true root cause. The actual issue reported may vary a little. There may be concerns that fridge temperatures are not taken, not recorded, recorded inconsistently, recorded as of concern with no action taken etc. The likelihood is high that most readers to this book have worked in a trust where some aspect of fridge temperatures has been reported as a concern by the CQC. You will know what solution you implemented for your trust and whether this had the desired effect or if this relatively small issue became a long-standing feature within regulatory reports for that trust. This specific concern can often prove to be a tricky one to resolve to the regulator's satisfaction. In such an event, the reason for this is that the trust in question has most likely failed to identify the root cause of their local variation. One could understand why an organisation might consider pulling a group together to undertake a RCA to be considered unnecessary for such a potentially very simple issue as recording fridge temperatures. However, without a RCA though one finds oneself with a vast array of potential solutions to set in train, with the potential for the selective blindness of an individual tasked with responsibility for addressing this concern to inform what solution will be identified and implemented. All potential solutions will likely appear logical and proportionate to interested parties and may represent legitimate contributory factors. Such solutions could include, replacing old fridges considered not to be working correctly, the removal of fridges no longer required, revising the existing policy and procedures for recording, reinforcing the mandatory requirement for senior nursing staff to record fridge temperatures, install an automatic system for recording temperatures, establishing regular audits of clinical areas, the options are almost endless and I've come across all of these solutions implemented in differing hospitals and all achieving very different results! It's not luck that some trusts address this issue swiftly and successfully, it's always because of an inclusive approach to explore the reasoning for this variation and the identification of an agreed solution to address the true root cause in that specific organisation. This is also why when some trusts choosing to replicate a solution implemented by another organisation to address the same problem do not always find that the same outcome is achieved. Returning to our painting analogy, the commendable approach to copying a masterpiece and seeking to replicate best practice elsewhere – a characteristic of a high performing organisation, is not going to be successful without the recognition that the best practice is not to be found in the solution implemented but the RAC undertaken to identify that solution.

The Potential Root-cause Have in Addressing Selective Blindness:

In an attempt to pull these threads together, we have recognised that trusts can be very good at identifying the root causes of a range of performance concerns but could benefit from explicitly defining the issue to be addressed as the locally identified root cause. This informing and education all stakeholders regarding the significance of the issue, generating a wider commitment for the maintenance of a prioritised focus. The practice of undertaking RCA to identify the systemic reasons for identified issues of concern needs to become routine so that rigour and challenge is applied to all potentially logical solutions proposed to address even the most seemingly straightforward of issues. The establishment of this routine practice of undertaking RCA and documenting these systemic issues will prevent wasted efforts being directed towards temporarily alleviating symptomatic issues and in turn strengthen the focus, momentum and sustainability of all improvements. Only in consistently undertake RCA can an organisation effectively remove any individual or internal selective blindness in an organisation and subsequently for the leaders in this organisation to be in a position themselves to call out and demand that selective blindness present in their stakeholders is also addressed. Clarification of root causes to be addressed that have impacted upon a range of symptomatic issues informs and educates external stakeholders to promote cooperation and collaboration. Equally, recognition that a wide range of initially unconnected symptomatic issues are the result of the cause and effect of a common root cause highlights the organisational importance of prioritising management action to rectify the systemic causes to realise the range of desired improvements. The identification of root causes directly within the influence of the organisation to address, will underpin the expectations of all stakeholders that improvements will be realised within a given timescale. Conversely, the identification of root causes NOT directly within the influence of the organisation to address, will underpin the expectations of the organisation that relevant stakeholders will take the necessary actions with the responsible parties to ensure external improvements are taken to ensure that the desired improvements within the trust are affected. Again, one must acknowledge and recognise the personal risk to any individual considering declining invitations to implement initiatives to address symptomatic issues and use the rationale as provided through a RCA to insist the efforts of all stakeholders remain focused on the actual root cause even when this is the responsibility of another party. It is not seeking to shift the blame or duck out of taking local actions necessary to improve performance but it is necessary to make any meaningful and sustainable improvements. Particularly in the scenario outlined in the first few pages of this book, the scenario of unacceptable ambulance response times due to ineffective in-patient flow throughout the hospital, the root cause being the increasing number of patients in acute beds waiting for transfer to an intermediate care or social care facility. In this scenario, which I personally view as germane to the future of the NHS as we have known it, the recognition and documentation of this root cause of a wide range of performance concerns currently experienced across acute care can only serve to inform, educate, explain and reinforce the necessity for those with the ability to directly influence this situation, to be held accountable to do so. Trusts can be held to account for delivering a range of initiatives designed to temporarily alleviate the symptoms, which may include the introduction of care coordinators, the expansion of virtual wards, a range of specialty based agreed pathways of care, or any other number of locally supported initiatives deemed to be logical, deliverable or that replicating being undertaken elsewhere with good effect. Hopefully you can see the recurring pitfalls here? Any of these commendable initiatives might have a positive impact for a discrete area of practice for a defined period, none will have the effect of sustainably improving the turnaround times of ambulances at A&E as none of these in any way seek to directly address the identified root cause being the limitations of social care. With the NHS viewed by many as being on its knees, NHS winter planning for 2022 having been initiated at the earliest point ever, during a prolonged heat wave, staff exhausted, and the workforce depleted, we need all stakeholders to recognise and focus upon the most significant systemic reasons for poor quality care and services. The overt use of RCA presents every single NHS organisation with a tool to contribute to insisting this of others and beginning to overcome the unacceptable degree of selective blindness that has been present for too long in those that oversee and are accountable for the performance of the NHS.

Chapter Summary

- The practice of undertaking RCA to identify the systemic reasons for identified issues of concern needs to become routine when developing organisational improvement plans, so that rigour and challenge is applied to all potentially logical solutions proposed to address even the most seemingly straightforward of issues.
- Recognised techniques to systematically explore all potential causes, using data to prioritise these to identify and document the root cause supports the development of a culture of continuous improvement.
- A SMART 'plus' action plan that identifies both the concerns initially identified and the root causes of those concerns may find that a common root cause has been identified for several issues. This emphasising the organisational significance of addressing the identified root cause as the reason for multiple symptomatic failings.
- The identification of root causes directly within the influence of the organisation to address, will underpin the expectations of all stakeholders to hold individuals to account that improvements will be realised within a given timescale.
- The identification of root causes NOT directly within the influence of the organisation to address, will underpin the expectations of the organisation that relevant stakeholders will take the necessary actions with the responsible parties to ensure external improvements are taken to ensure that the desired improvements within the trust are affected.
- The overt use of RCA presents every single NHS organisation with a tool to contribute to insisting this of others and beginning to overcome the unacceptable degree of selective blindness that has been present for too long in those that oversee and are accountable for the performance of the NHS.

Chapter 8
Developing Internal Independence

In May 2019, I wrote an article published in the Health Service Journal (HSJ), titled *The NHS has suffered a critical loss of authentic internal challenge*[8]. I was in the middle of my tenure working for the CQC as National Professional Adviser – Well Led Reviews. I had been involved directly and indirectly with numerous leadership reviews in every type of trust across the country. In this article, I shared my observation that the undesirable aspects of familiarity and self-review had seemingly become central to the approach being taken across the NHS in evaluating the delivery and impact of improvement plans. I offered the recommendation that to strengthen assurance arrangements, responsibility for evaluating the delivery of an improvement plan should be given to a different individual from that responsible for the development and delivery of that plan. The intent of this recommendation was to increase the degree of independence present within a process of developing and delivering any type of improvement plan. This chapter continues to explore the very prevalent risks posed by advocacy and self-interest and the perfect storm that can be created if selective blindness also features in this mix. The detrimental impact this can have on rigour, objectivity and the generation of reassurance rather than assurance affecting significantly the delivery of any improvement plan. I aim to highlight the significance of developing a healthy degree of internal independence, the potential ways of achieving this and the benefits for trusts in developing grip, momentum and sustainability of their improvements.

The Challenges of Helping and Supporting an Executive Lead:

Portfolios are often extensive and complex for those given a lead responsibility for quality; this involving directing, leading, supporting, evaluating quality improvements across services and generating information for others that provides assurance of progress. At a strategic level, the organisational remit is usually shared by the trust board executive Nurse and Medical directors. Whilst the clinical rational for this is sound, such arrangements can present a risk to objectivity which should be more widely recognised and could be mitigated through the establishment of some consistent arrangements designed to introduce and develop a degree of internal independence.

The portfolio of an executive lead for quality, which is frequently the board nurse, often involves specific responsibility for developing a quality strategy, for establishing an organisational approach to improvement and developing a prioritised and detailed trust wide improvement plan. Responsibility also routinely includes liaising directly with regulators, leading on the undertaking of all inspections and the preparation of responses to regulatory reports and findings. In terms of reporting on progress, one might also expect to find the executive lead to have responsibility for managing a central team supporting improvement work, this including the preparation of reports on delivery to operational groups, assurance committees, the trust board, commissioners and external stakeholders. These aspects of the responsibilities as an executive lead represent a huge portfolio. What such an extensive portfolio of responsibility can mean is that the executive lead directly signs off the detail of an improvement plan, seeking support organisationally to deliver that plan. Following endorsement of the plan the executive lead then endorses specific initiatives and oversees the implementation of these to deliver the entire plan, in addition to personally evaluating the extent and success of the delivery. At regular intervals and in response to ad hoc requests for progress updates, the executive lead also prepares and endorses internal and external reports for stakeholders to offer assurance of progress. Whilst the knowledge and expertise of the executive lead is unquestionable, like any of us an executive lead may have areas of conscious or unconscious selective blindness. Recognising the potential of selective blindness in any individual should support the consideration of proactive steps to be taken to mitigate such risks. The agreement of some simple adjustments to create some opportunities for developing a degree of internal independence and constructive challenge at differing stages of the quality improvement cycle should be viewed as a positive approach to supporting the organisation with the generation of robust assurance of progress.

Accepting the Need to Develop Independence:

Later chapters will explore other opportunities for strengthening assurance arrangements at both an operational and strategic level, which should be considered in addition to strengthening the organisations potential for developing internal independence to promote objectivity and rigour of evaluation and assessment.

The approach that an organisation adopts to building in internal independence into its quality improvement cycle should be viewed as appropriately being as potentially as varied as the nature of differing trusts. It will be important that all aspects of any approach taken are open and transparent so that they are likely to be viewed as professionally acceptable by all members of the senior leadership team; in addition to being pragmatic and sufficiently flexible to allow for appropriate adjustments to accommodate conflicting organisational pressures, when this presents as being in the organisation's best interest. Given this, it would be appropriate for any arrangements put into place to be widely vary across differing trusts to reflect the different nature of teams and roles in place to support improvement work. The differing opportunities for developing internal independence in organisations are virtually endless. It is important to recognise though that however robust you might consider your local arrangements to be in offering a consistently objective approach to improving services, that there will always be opportunities able to be identified and explored as to how this degree of objectivity can be further strengthened. Before we go any further, I would like to invite you to take this moment to consider your initial response to the implied need for your organisation to mitigate potential risks of advocacy, self-review and selective blindness. Was your reaction representative of a high performing organisation including humility and the drive to improve further, or possibly more indicative of a struggling organisation denying that there is any need?

So, let's begin to explore where some of the obvious opportunities are for developing internal independence and the degree of constructive challenge present within a quality improvement cycle. In the previous chapter we explored the challenges of developing a SMART 'plus' action plan, particularly focusing on the need to identify the systemic true root causes of concerns to allow for sustainable solutions to be realised. There will be many potential opportunities for encouraging challenge and contributions from differing perspectives through the promotion of processes that ensure a dynamic dialogue between corporate and clinical teams is promoted to foster a widespread confidence in all elements of the developed plan.

Opportunities for Viewing Constructive Conflict Positively:

At the point immediately prior to the presenting the developed plan to the organisation for endorsement, lies the first significant opportunity for an organisation to take a proactive approach to developing internal independence and establishing an invitation for constructive challenge. An option being for a senior individual who has not been directly involved in the development process to date to be identified as a collaborator to generate a degree of constructive conflict, by being invited to give some focused time to comprehensively review the plan, this with the aim of identifying any inconsistencies, potential conflicts, points requiring clarification, potential inaccuracies and any obvious errors. Given the size and detail of many improvement plans, undertaking such a 'fresh eyes' review will require sufficient time to be carved out of a potentially busy diary but there is always the potential for such an individual to be external to the organisation if this is considered necessary to not put further pressure on heavy internal workloads. This is a role I've been asked to take on by several trusts, and without needing to know any of the detail of how the trusts performs, the insight a pair of fresh eyes can offer should not be underestimated. For those of you who are questioning the necessity for such a review, I would simply offer that I am always able when given a trust's improvement plan for the first time, to identify very easily if such an independent review has been internally undertaken by an organisation. When this has taken place, such a plan is coherent, consistent and provides immediate clarity of intention and approach. Where such an independent review has not taken place, the plan invariably generates for a new reader a raft of questions about aspects of the plan requiring considerable clarification. This new reader could be an individual like myself working with the senior leadership team, an external stakeholder or an internal committee considering the plan for the first time. If this sort of dialogue and reaction is one that resonates with you when having presented plans for endorsement within your organisation, you might find it very helpful to change this reaction and dynamic by identifying an individual who could act as a critical friend at the point suggested in your ongoing development process. The significant commitment of time from a single reviewer to act in this capacity will prove to be very time efficient for everyone else involved in the development and review process as the accuracy and the interpretation of the plan's contents become more consistent, enabling discussions to focus on issues of greatest organisational importance. If there is confidence at this stage regarding the nature of RCA undertaken and the degree of collective agreement in the identification of root causes, the pace of improvements will gather quickly, and momentum build consistently. Recognising the time commitment being sought for fresh eyes comprehensive review of a plan, one also doesn't need to have the same critical friend at this stage. Inviting differing individuals to undertake this role shares the load as well as offering potential development opportunities for senior colleagues who otherwise wouldn't be directly involved in this work.

Opportunities for Ensuring Robust Evidence Underpins Judgements:

The next significant opportunity for an organisation to take a proactive approach to developing internal independence presents itself in terms of assessing the relevance and strength of the information internally identified as evidence of progress of delivery of initiatives to address root causes identified and or the achievement of the outcomes sought. Information being presented as evidential will invariably take differing forms e.g., reports, audit findings. They may also be proposed from a wide variety of sources and potentially via colleagues with widely differing levels of understanding regarding the issue of concern or the initiatives taken to reduce variation. This is not a criticism, simply an inevitability given the complexities of trust workings. This reality does present a risk though, necessitating a forensic review of all submitted information prior to recognising and recording this as evidence. Without fail in every improvement plan review that I have ever been involved with, working in any of my differing capacities, I have been presented without exception with erroneous or inappropriate examples of information provided by a trust to supposedly evidence the successful implementation to a previously identified concern. Such examples may simply be weak, or more concerningly demonstrate a lack of understanding of the concern required to be addressed. Occasionally they prove to have no relevance at all to the issue in question. Given the size and complexities of some organisational improvement plans and the volume of evidence that can potentially be gathered and offered to demonstrate improvements that have been made, a small number of such inappropriate items of information may be accepted as administrative errors, particularly if accompanied with other appropriate evidence that is directly relevant to the issue of concern, the identified root cause and the outcomes being sought. However, where such inappropriate information is presented alone to evidence delivery of a specific issue or is presented to support evidence of delivery for several elements of an action plan, this can evidence a significant risk to the achievement of an organisation's strategic aims and objectives which we will expand upon further when we explore the importance of defining strategic assurance levels. A simple example of this was from a trust that was required by the regulator to standardise practice relating to the management of post-operative nausea. The trust's response was to swiftly evidence the existence of such a long-standing policy; rate the action as green and immediately close the issue of concern. The policy evidence supplied by the trust failed to demonstrate an authentic exploration of this concern, overlooking the issues that given that this response was factually accurate, staff either weren't aware of the existence of this policy or chose not to follow it. In the absence of any independent challenge at this stage and organisational acceptance that this concern had been fully addressed, this issue would likely be raised specifically again by the regulator as part of a future inspection in addition to other concerns being raised of symptomatic failings arising from the organisational root cause which was something to do with policy awareness and implementation. In this example, the organisation had sought a comprehensive audit to be undertaken of the status of their reported improvement plan and although were surprised at the challenge provided on this issue, they welcomed the opportunity to revisit this initial concern to identify the real root cause of this and take appropriate actions to ensure sustainable improvement. In this example, because of undertaking an RCA on this issue, the systemic cause relating to a fundamental disconnect between policy development and corporate cascade arrangements to communicate policy developments were recognised as causing the symptomatic effect reported by regulator. This root cause requiring some fundamental systematic initiatives to be actioned and audited over time to generate sufficient evidence for this concern to be evaluated as addressed. For a trust to choose to take a proactive approach to identifying an internal or external critical friend to read and evaluate all submitted information prior to recognising such information as evidencing progress will significantly mitigate the risks of the usual internal focus being on coordinating the recording and presentation of information. It is easy for enthusiastic teams who wish to evidence the efforts that have been made to improve services, to promote quantity of information rather than the quality of evidence. It is also understandable given the complexity of some improvement plans and the significance of some of the root causes they are seeking to address, that some more discrete issues of concern are considered to be easily addressed, with the potential for these issues to be misjudged and their significance overlooked. An effective internal critical friend does not need to have any in depth knowledge of the issue of concern, just be able to commit the time to review every item of potential evidence to assess its relevance and strength. This step often being missed in the challenge of operational colleagues being required to provide updates of progress in addition to delivering on the day job! A critical friend can significantly contribute to the removal of inappropriate information and the development and revision of information to increase its value as evidence. This exercise also not required to be undertaken solely by a single individual, with colleagues from differing clinical teams pragmatically able to act in this capacity for each other. This simple adjustment of the time already was taken by individuals to generate and submit potential evidence to support an assessment of progress, significantly strengthening the rigour with which information generated and the consistency of that information as well as minimising any potential selective blindness that may be influencing this specific aspect of the plan.

Opportunities for Strengthening Organisational Assurance Processes:

The remaining two most significant opportunities for developing internal independence relate to reviewing the operational assessment of delivery that an organisation makes as an important element of generating organisational assurance and the reporting of that level of assurance to trust board assurance sub committees. Whilst both areas are critical elements of a strong assurance framework and therefore will be explored in detail later on, we will continue here to recognise the potential that these additional opportunities offer to organisations willing to adjust existing arrangements to safeguarding themselves against potential risks of selective blindness, advocacy and self-interest. Once an organisation has generated evidence of implementation of a range of initiatives believed to have addressed initial concerns and the root cause of these concerns, an evaluation is undertaken to summarise this position. As we have acknowledged when considering the scope of historical SMART action plans, these action plan evaluations have been largely reflected in the form of a simple three level red, amber, green (RAG) summary rating. The simplicity of this rating might not unreasonably support the assumption that there will be a consistent interpretation made of these ratings. It is not however my experience that this can be relied upon to be the case. Does green reflect an evaluation that everything is actioned as intended or that the desired outcome has been achieved? Does amber simply reflect that the timescale set for completion of actions has not yet been reached, reflecting work in progress or does it reflect that there is concern that timescales have slipped? Does red indicate that initiatives have not been implemented as intended or that they have not resulted in the expected impact or outcome? Hopefully, in the posing of three generic simple questions one can appreciate the potential for evaluations using this approach to be inconsistent and too easily influenced by any selective blindness present in the individual providing the evaluation, in addition to being influenced by advocacy if the individual undertaking the evaluation is evaluating initiatives, they have also been responsible for implementing. Some trusts have recognised the need to provide simple definitions for the elements of the RAG rating used, with the aim of promoting consistency. Some have helpfully introduced additional elements to clarify when initiatives have not yet commenced or indeed are completed in full. Implementing a seven-stepped approach to evaluating operational delivery of an improvement plan I have seen make a huge difference to the operational traction an organisation can achieve in delivering its improvement priorities and we will explore this approach in considerable detail in the next chapter. The important issue for us to consider now, is that regardless of the level of detail being taken by an organisation to evaluate progress, internal independence can be strengthened at this stage by again identifying an internal independent party to consider the indicative RAG rating awarded to a set of initiatives, reviewing these to ensure that ratings are being consistently applied and reflective of the endorsed evidence available.

Do We Realistically Have the Luxury of Time Available to Do These Things?

I appreciate that you may be thinking all this additional activity of undertaking independent reviews will require time which will add in pressure to already pressurised workloads whilst potentially slowing down the process for updating and reporting upon the plan. This is certainly a risk that one would wish to mitigate and agreeing an internal reporting process that possibly focuses on elements rather than the entire plan so that the quality of the plan's evaluation is itself significantly strengthened to provide operational assurance of implementation will reduce duplication, requests for clarification and challenges from stakeholders overseeing the delivery of the plan. This example of potentially developing internal independence mirrors the opportunity posed by the requirement to provide reports to trust board sub committees the present assurance of both delivery and progress. Again, the historically used three levels of assurance, red usually indicating no assurance, amber representing some degree of partial assurance and green representing assurance, presents the same challenges of interpretation and potential inconsistency of use. At a strategic level using three levels of assurance usually result in an amber rating being used most consistently, with the significance of this often not identified or recognised. Once more, as this is a critical element of a strong assurance framework which we will be looking at in greater detail, but for now, again regardless of the number or definitions of the strategic ratings being used, an invitation to a senior executive or deputy not directly responsible for this portfolio of work to present an assurance report generated by the executive lead would offer a significant opportunity for executive challenge to be required to occur PRIOR to committee discussions, providing the opportunity to clarify and strengthen reports to ensure best use of committee time to focus on the significance of any outstanding managerial action. Formally utilising an executive other than the executive lead offers the additional potential of leveraging their areas of expertise to strengthen both the evaluation and conclusions drawn and the presentation of reports which can often focus on presenting detail rather than explaining the findings. In my experience, anything that assists in strengthening the digestibility of assurance papers is usually very much appreciated by committee members!

Will It Be Worth It?

As indicated, these four main points in the improvement cycle offer clear opportunities for establishing and developing a degree of internal independence which rather than requiring significant additional time to be found, more pragmatically required the invitation to be extended to colleagues not routinely engaged in these activities to act as a critical friend. The aim of this being to strengthen both the consistency of the plan's content, the evidence identified to support the evaluation of progress, the consistency of evaluation applied, and the nature of assurance generated. Wider benefits are also able to be realised, in terms of improved use of committee time to focus less on points of correction and clarification, focusing more on discussions regarding outstanding management action required in response to assurance provided. This presented the potential of a significant organisational improvement of the level of grip, momentum of progress and the sustainability of improvements being achieved across the organisation.

Chapter Summary

The strengthening of internal independence to mitigate the risk of familiarisation and self-review is possible for all trusts regardless of the level of confidence held in existing arrangements. Rather than requiring the commitment of more time, considering pragmatic adjustments to existing processes can offer significant improvements to the consistency of improvement plans, the rigour with which their delivery is evaluated and the confidence in the level of assurance available, plus the impact and use of available assurance committee time and expertise.

Whilst the options for developing internal independence will be as varied as the number of trusts providing services, four primary opportunities have been identified:

- The introduction of a critical friend to review the improvement plan prior to organisational endorsement. This review to address potential inconsistencies, conflicts, inaccuracies or errors.
- The use of colleagues to review the relevance and strength of all information submitted to be considered as evidence of improvement.
- The identification of an individual to provide independent challenge, review and endorsement of indicative evaluations of progress made.
- The use of an alternative executive to finalise and present to the assurance committee the strategic progress report provided by the executive lead.

Wider benefits from this approach can be seen in terms of improved use of committee time to focus less on points of correction and clarification, supporting greater focus of discussions regarding outstanding management action required in response to assurance provided. The outcome of this being an improvement of the level of grip, momentum of progress and the sustainability of improvements being achieved across the organisation.

Chapter 9
Seven Steps to Operational Assurance

Within our detailed exploration of SMART 'plus' improvement plans and the importance that has been placed on undertaking an effective process for developing such a plan, significant emphasis has been placed upon including the undertaking of RCA for each identified concern, so that plans include initiatives identified to both address the symptomatic concerns in addition to the more important underlying systemic reasons for those concerns. We have additionally described explicit opportunities and some options for developing internal independence so that regardless of the level of detail being taken by an organisation to evaluate progress, the invitation to a critical friend to review these will ensure that the rating levels being used by a trust are being consistently applied and reflective of the endorsed evidence available.

What are the Limitations of a Traditional RAG Rating?

Despite the best of intentions, it is not possible for a simple three level RAG rating to summarise a comprehensive evaluation of progress that should reflect the minimum evaluation of delivery and progress as referenced to:

- The impact of initiatives undertaken on the symptom of the issue.
- The effectiveness of initiatives designed to address the systemic reason for that symptom.
- The achievement of the outcome desired over a period of time.

The restriction of three levels fails to provide the necessary granularity to reflect the above three issues in sufficient detail and is the reason why more levels are required to offer a desirable degree of operational assurance of progress. It is strongly advocated that seven levels of evaluation to be used to summarise operational delivery at this operational micro level. The potential visual comparison of the historically used RAG levels against a more detailed seven level evaluation framework being presented below.

Operational Delivery Evaluation Levels	
Historical RAG rating	Recommended seven levels
	Level 7
	Level 6
	Level 5
	Level 4
	Level 3
	Level 2
	Level 1
	Level 0

This representation demonstrates the potential for greater discernment and granularity of evaluation when using seven levels, which although is not in itself surprising, using the simplest of interpretations of red being undesirable and green being desirable, it is significant that the threshold for determining what is desirable or undesirable in delivery terms differs across the two approaches. It is this difference that I have found to be of greatest help to operational teams in focusing improvement efforts and promoting sustainable improvement. The reason for this, needs to be described and explained fully.

What Do Each of the Seven Levels Specifically Represent?

Each of the seven Levels of operational evaluation refers to three key aspects of delivery. These was, to describe in detail initiatives/actions identified to address concerns, the identification and addressing of underlying causes and the measurement of desired outcomes. To demonstrate and describe this in detail for each specific level:

Levels 0: Rated RED; reflects the start of a plan's development with emerging actions not yet agreed with all relevant parties and there understandably being no evident improvements identified. In simple terms, level 0 can represent a commendable organisational enthusiasm and appetite to improve, recognition and commitment to develop a comprehensive plan and considerable engagement and efforts to record and agree the detail of such a plan but at this stage, no evidence progressed in agreeing or delivering a plan.

Level 1: Also rated RED; reflects that Initial actions to directly address specific symptomatic performance concerns have been agreed upon, with desired outcomes being in the process of being defined. Again, at this level there are understandably still no evident improvements identified. In simple terms, level 1 indicates commendable practical coordination of efforts towards the agreement and delivery of a plan.

Level 2: The last of the RED levels, reflects that comprehensive actions to directly address specific symptomatic performance concerns have been identified and agreed upon, with some impact evident from these actions able to be measured. In simple terms, level 2 indicates positive development and agreement of an initial plan that focuses on the symptomatic issues of concern.

Progress through the RED levels 0–2 reflects a logical and desirable initial progression of insight and understanding necessary to develop an improvement plan. Whilst it may be considered desirable and usual that progression through these levels takes place at pace, it is worthy of noting that the commonality that determines the RED levels 0–2, is the absence of the undertaking of RCA and the failure to formally recognise all contributory causes and the systemic cause of any variation.

Levels 3: Rated AMBER, reflecting the significance of the undertaking of a RCA to identify the systemic causes/reasons for performance variation. At this level, comprehensive actions have been identified and agreed upon to address both the symptomatic performance concerns, the contributory causes and the root cause of these issues. This level represents the existence of some measurable impact evident from actions taken and an emerging clarity of outcomes sought to determine sustainability. Level 3 offers agreed measures to evidence improvement.

Levels 4: Also rated AMBER, reflecting level 3 in terms of the undertaking of a RCA to identify the of systemic causes/reasons for performance variation, with comprehensive actions identified and agreed upon to address both the symptomatic performance concerns and the root causes of these issues. This difference between level 3 and 4 being that level 4 represents evidence of an increased number of agreed actions being delivered, but these still at this point, with little or no evidence of the achievement of desired outcomes.

Levels 5: The unexpected level rated RED, again reflects the undertaking of a RCA to identify the of systemic causes/reasons for performance variation, with comprehensive actions identified and agreed upon to address both the symptomatic performance concerns and the root causes as in levels 3 and 4. This difference between level 5 and the other amber levels representing a further increasing degree to which actions have now been delivered, with level 5 representing the majority of all agreed actions evidenced as delivered, but still little or no evidence of the delivery of the desired outcome. It is important to recognise that if a number of initiatives have been successfully implemented to address a range of identified causes, with no desired outcome being realised, it is likely that the correct root cause has not been identified requiring the RCA to be revisited. This is the rationale for identifying this level as RED. It would be expected to see priority management intervention and action being taken in response to this rating.

The commonality that determines the AMBER levels 3–5, being the increasing implementation of agreed actions, accompanied by the absence of any significant evidence of these actions achieving the desired outcomes sought.

Level 6: Is rated GREEN, representing actions to address both specific and underlying causes for variance being in an advanced stage of delivery, with emerging evidence of the achievement of desired outcomes. This evidence that the correct identification of the true root cause of the issue of concern will still require a continuation of this approach to be maintained to ensure improvements are embedded and the improvement outcome being sought is realised.

The final level 7 is rated BLUE representing achievement of a sustained improvement, with evidence of delivery of the majority or all of the agreed actions and clear evidence of the achievement of desired outcomes that has been sustained over a defined period of time i.e., three months. It would be considered appropriate for there to be confidence for ongoing performance management of issues evaluated at this level to transfer to 'business as usual'.

A summary of these definitions is provided in the table below:

RAG rating	ACTIONS	OUTCOMES
Level 7	Comprehensive actions identified/agreed to address specific performance concerns AND recognition of systemic causes/reasons for variation.	Evidence of delivery of the majority or all of the agreed actions, with clear evidence of the achievement of desired outcomes over a defined period of time i.e., three months.

Level 6	Comprehensive actions identified/agreed to address specific performance concerns AND recognition of systemic causes/reasons for variation.	Evidence of delivery of the majority or all of the agreed actions, with clear evidence of the achievement also of desired outcomes.
Level 5	Comprehensive actions identified/agreed to address specific performance concerns AND recognition of systemic causes/reasons for variation.	Evidence of delivery of the majority or all of the agreed actions, with little or no evidence of the achievement of desired outcomes.
Level 4	Comprehensive actions identified/agreed to address specific performance concerns AND recognition of systemic causes/reasons for variation.	Evidence of several agreed actions being delivered, with little or no evidence of the achievement of desired outcomes.
Level 3	Comprehensive actions identified/agreed to address specific performance concerns AND recognition of systemic causes/reasons for variation.	Some measurable impact evident from actions initially taken AND an emerging clarity of outcomes sought to determine sustainability, with agreed measures to evidence improvement.
Level 2	Comprehensive actions identified/agreed upon to address specific concerns.	Some measurable impact evident from actions initially taken.
Level 1	Initial actions agreed, focused upon directly addressing specific concerns.	Outcomes sought being defined. No improvements yet evident.

| Level 0 | Emerging actions not yet agreed. | No improvements evident. |

How Does Using This Seven-step Framework Help to Drive Improvement?

An increasing number of trusts are recognising the need to increase the differentiation of their operational evaluations of improvement delivery to help in focusing efforts. Those trusts which have embraced the principles of these seven-stepped approaches have found that the consistency and clarity that these clearly defined levels provide to all colleagues involved in improving services helps significantly in collaboratively focusing efforts towards supporting implementation and the refinement and adjustment of plans if necessary. The clear criteria for each level significantly reduces the element of personal judgement influencing the determination of the evaluation rating and counters any potential aspects of selective blindness present within those responsible for determining ratings. Specifically applying a seven-level evaluation framework in the trust that had 77 separate action plans was viewed as contributing significantly to generating a focus on the basics required to drive improvement and has remained a foundation of their approach to improvement as their performance has gone from strength to strength. Seven levels of evaluation provide a framework to support a logical sequence of efforts that will ensure a balanced development of all aspects of an improvement plan. It will for example, be clear to all colleagues that the elements of a plan that are rated RED from 0–2 will need to immediately prioritise the undertaking of RCA to agree and confirm the systemic causes of variation. The granularity of three differing AMBER levels 3–5 equally allows for the swift identification of any significant delay of deterioration of delivery of outcomes, which in turn will call into question the extent of the RCA undertaken and the accuracy of the root cause identified; suggesting that these aspects be revisited. It is also significant that there is only one GREEN level 6 within this framework representing the significance of the delivery of desired outcomes. The importance at this level being to determine what timescale for sustaining this level of improvement will constitutes a 'closing' of this aspect of the plan through the reaching the only BLUE level 7 which represents sustainable improvement and marks the organisational achievement of 'business as usual'.

Chapter Summary

Recognising the risks to applying a simple three level RAG rating to summarise an evaluation of progress, the use of seven levels of operational evaluation framework to evaluate and summarise operational delivery of an improvement plan at a micro level has proved to be highly effective in reducing the element of personal judgement and countering any potential aspects of selective blindness present. Achieving this by each of the levels referring to three key aspects of delivery:

- The detail of initiatives/actions identified to address concerns.
- The identification and addressing of underlying causes.
- The measurement of desired outcomes.

Trusts applying the granularity of evaluation offered within the seven levels have significantly strengthened the consistency of evaluations undertaken and increased the focus towards supporting implementation and the refinement and adjustment of plans if identified as necessary. The granularity of the levels supports the prioritisation of the undertaking of RCA to agree and confirm the systemic causes of variation and equally allows for the swift identification of any significant delay of deterioration of delivery of outcomes. The focus on evaluating outcomes calls into question the extent of the RCA undertaken and need for these aspects to be revisited where outcomes are not being achieved as desired. The significance of the delivery of desired outcomes is represented by the single GREEN level within this framework representing the achievement of these. The seventh, final and optimal level, represented sustainable improvement of these outcomes and the formal transfer of ongoing performance management to business as usual.

Chapter 10
Defining Strategic Assurance Levels

What Is Assurance Industry Best Practice?

Just as has become the historical norm across the NHS for the use of a simple three-level RAG rating for evaluating delivery of improvements at an operational level, has this approach been replicated by most trusts when evaluating the level of organisational assurance available. Although the replicated use of a three-level RAG rating for both operational implementation and strategic assurance may suggest a consistency of approach which might be considered advantageous, in reality, it presents an inconsistency of approach regarding how assurance is measured across the NHS where this is undertaken and provided by independent external parties. In these circumstances' assurance is usually being sought to be generated on a macro basis, to evidence the delivery or implementation of a wide range of initiatives or standards for a complex portfolio of work. This might represent the delivery of wide-ranging services or the achievement of delivering an organisations improvement plan. These independent parties could be regulatory in nature such as the CQC; represent a national office for inspection such as Ofsted or represent an organisation's appointed external auditor. All such external bodies undertaking inspections, audits or reviews of services of aspects of service provision are found to use current 'best practice' regarding defining assurance levels to confirm to the organisation their observations and findings that underpin the assurance level they provide to the organisation regarding the quality of services provided. Existing recognised best practice defines four levels of principle judgements of assurance to be the most effective number to be used, not 3. The primary reason for this being that in using only three levels of evaluation, the middle level is the one found to be identified most frequently when making an assessment. In the scenario where there is a choice of three levels, where one extreme represents optimum/ideal standards and the other extreme represents unacceptable standards, it is not unreasonable to anticipate that majority of evaluation of standards will lie somewhere between these two positions. The main limitations of this approach being that a single middle level of assessment offers little indication of the significance of the rationale for this assessment, which in turn offers little help in determining the priority of any outstanding managerial actions that may be considered necessary to improve performance and the likelihood of improving future evaluations.

What Is Regulatory Assurance Best Practice?

Interestingly, both the CQC and Ofsted who have adopted recognised best practice of determining four levels of assurance, describe their levels of assurance using the same terms. The lowest of these evaluations being 'inadequate', the next being 'requires improvement', the next being 'good' and the best being 'outstanding'. The use of these four descriptors makes it very clear where the acceptable standard of assurance lies; this being at the specific point between the second and third levels. This explicit point representing the difference between what is evaluated as considered to be acceptable and what is not. Using four levels of assurance in this way provides absolute clarity on the significance of improvements required, leaving an organisation in no doubt of the significance of any identified outstanding management action. To explore this further, whilst an organisation given a regulatory rating of 'good' may still be required to address outstanding areas of concern and be expected to take additional managerial action to achieve this, the organisation may be confident that the interpretation of the 'good' rating received confirms to the organisation that any improvement requirements are not considered by the regulator to present any significant risks or are considered to be vital to the achievement of the organisation's strategic objectives. This regulatory assurance rating does also make clear to the organisation that it is considered that failure to address these requirements could lead to an increase in the likelihood of risk to achieving the organisation's strategic objectives and therefore any necessary management actions identified as part of this assurance level should not be ignored.

The use of best practice by regulators in using four explicit and clearly defined definitions of the quality of services assured helpfully presents little scope for interpretation. The use of explicit standards, the formation of judgements based upon triangulated evidence and the reporting of findings using defined language promoting a consistency of interpretation and understanding that supports the development of a timely and appropriate organisational response to be made.

What Can We Learn from the Language Used By External Auditors?

External auditors who similarly recognise the use of four levels often use very similar terms to define these four levels; terms such as the lowest being no assurance, the next being partial assurance, the next being significant assurance, with the final being full assurance. Without exception, external auditors will all have detailed definitions of each level that refer to all aspects of the controls being evaluated and how these relate to levels of organisational risk. This is in marked contrast to common practice across the NHS where we find trusts that rarely stray from the three most basic descriptors of no assurance, partial assurance and full assurance: it is even rarer to find trusts having detailed definitions to explain the use of these three terms. Given the scope and complexity of the trust wide improvement programmes, being evaluated by assurance sub committees at a macro strategic level, the absence of detailed definitions that seek to explicitly describe the interdependent relationship between the delivery of agreed improvement initiatives, the achievement of strategic objectives and the prioritisation of management capacity, make it very difficult for members of the senior leadership team to consistently interpret the significance of assurance levels reported. Using the same rationale that we used to critique the simple three-level RAG rating to summarise an evaluation of operational implementation, a three-level RAG to summarise available organisational assurance progress will also fail to sufficiently provide a granularity of assessment of the information available to evidence successful strategic macro implementation of an improvement plan evaluated using the detail described within the seven levels.

What are the Levels of Strategic Assurance?

At such a strategic macro level, where the assurance available needs to be measured against the organisation's strategic objectives, the risks to achieving these objectives and the significance of managerial action required to be taken to mitigate these risks, the recognised best practice of defining and utilising four levels of strategic assurance is recommended to be used. A visual representative comparison of the historically used three RAG levels against the recommended 4 level red, amber, green, blue RAGB is presented below.

Area of concern	Strategic Assurance Levels		Point of concern
	Historic RAG used	Recommended Best Practice RAGB	
↑↓	Fully Assured	Full Assurance	←
		Significant Assurance	
	Partial Assurance	Partial Assurance	
		No Assurance	
	No Assurance		

Again, this representation demonstrates the potential for greater discernment and granularity of evaluation when using four levels rather than three. It is not as simple though as just adding in an extra level within a BRAB assurance evaluation. The introduction of an additional level of granularity does have the effect of adjusting the historical RAG thresholds for determining what may be viewed as highly undesirable or providing no assurance and that which may be considered highly desirable or providing full assurance. It is this refinement of what is explicitly acceptable and unacceptable which really can offer a trust board and it's assurance sub committees a further mechanism for reducing the degree to which personal judgement influences the level of assurance identified and mitigating any potential of selective blindness present within key individuals. This approach presenting much needed clarity and focus on the areas being reported to committees, which in turn inform the areas requiring explanation, discussion and decisions to be made.

Also specifically identified in the table above for the three-level RAG assurance is the potential range of organisational concern that is a direct consequence of not having the clarity of the significance of any assessment evaluated as amber and providing partial assurance. This is not only an unhelpfully wide potential range of concerns, but in the absence of detailed definitions of what partial assurance means, will require considerable enquiry and exploration to identify and agree the significance of this evaluation. This scenario can often be played out repeatedly in committee meetings, focusing the time and energy of all members in discussions that at best can provide some reassurance of efforts being made as opposed to evidencing assurance of progress. In contrast, the benefits of the four-level RAGB assurance are rooted in the identification of a specific point of organisational concern between the evaluation of green, significant assurance and amber for partial assurance: it is at this point that the detailed definitions identify that the organisation should be concerned and the trust board become directly engaged in ensuring appropriate management action is taken to mitigate the explicitly identified risks recognised as impacting upon the achievement of the organisation's strategic objectives. The specific point of this occurrence may be considered by some members to be restrictive and possibly unfair in some scenarios but again the specific definition this point represents serves to effectively remove the application of personal judgement and safeguard against individual selective blindness that may seek for a more flexible interpretation of the assurance levels and an inconsistent decision reached regarding the level of assurance demonstrated.

What Do Detailed Definitions of Assurance Need to Include?

To promote consistency of understanding, application and interpretation of strategic assurance levels, trusts should commit to detailed definitions that explain and underpin the rationale for each level of assurance. Such definitions should explicitly refer to the design and effective operation of the existing system (for improvement) and controls in place, impact upon the achievement of the organisation's strategic objectives, the risks to the organisation's reputation or other strategic risks and finally the significance of any managerial action identified as required to be taken. The table below offers clear definitions of each of the recommended 4 levels of strategic assurance for a trust to use to underpin its evaluation and interpretation of progress.

Assurance	Description
Full Assurance	<ul><li>The system design and existing controls are working well.</li><li>Potential innovations being considered all relate to achieving recognised best practice.</li></ul>
Significant Assurance – with minor improvement opportunities	<ul><li>The system design and existing controls are working well.</li><li>Some minor improvements have been identified.</li><li>Identified management actions are not considered vital to achievement of strategic aims & objectives – although if unaddressed may increase likelihood of risk.</li></ul>
Partial Assurance – with improvements required	<ul><li>The system design and existing controls require strengthening in areas.</li><li>A few operational weaknesses have been recognised.</li><li>Existing performance presents some areas of concern regarding exposure to reputational or other strategic risks.</li></ul>

	• Weaknesses identified present an unacceptable level of risk to achieving strategic aims and objectives. • A small number of priority management actions have been accepted as urgently required.
No Assurance	• The system design and existing controls are ineffective. • Several fundamental operational weaknesses have been recognised. • Existing performance presents an unacceptable exposure to reputational or other strategic risks. • Weaknesses identified are directly impacting upon the prevention to achieving strategic aims and objectives. • Several priority management actions have been accepted as urgently required.

To develop an appreciation of the significance of the definitions offered above, let's explore some of the scenarios that might warrant the application of these terms.

What Is the Significance of the Definition of 'No Assurance?'

The lowest of these assurance levels represented as RED and providing no assurance, could be used to reflect a range of scenarios. The first could relate to a complex improvement plan not being delivered as intended, with either several agreed timescales for actions being missed or the failure to realise expected outcomes. In this scenario the most logical response might involve seeking an independent critical friend to review the existing SMART action plan to provide assurance that it is sufficiently SMART 'plus'. Alternatively, if there was confidence that the action plan in place was SMART 'plus', exploring opportunities for locally strengthening the degree if internal independence available to support the evaluation of evidence of progress being made, might also offer new insights into adjustments necessary to increase the focus or momentum of improvement work. In the event that assurance of progress was expected, but not available, an urgent collaboration with a critical friend to generate an effective degree of constructive conflict to identify why this has occurred would certainly seem to be advantageous. It is important reminder though, that the reporting of no assurance for a portfolio of work does not indicate that no progress has been made or that there aren't elements of assurance available to evidence elements of progress. No assurance does importantly provide an overall macro summary of the assurance available to an organisation regarding a significant aspect of the organisation's performance. No assurance does clearly identify that within a given portfolio of work there are several areas that have been identified as presenting an *unacceptable* exposure to reputational or other organisational strategic risks. In this scenario it would be expected for these issues to be immediately escalated to the trust board so that necessary priority executive and managerial actions are identified and agreed.

What Is the Significance of the Definition of 'Partial Assurance – with Improvements Required'?

The next level up is represented as AMBER and providing partial assurance – with improvements required. Again, the reasons for this could relate to a complex improvement plan not being delivered as intended, with the significant difference at this level being recognition that there are only a few areas of concern where progress or delivery has not been evaluated as intended. Given the focused areas of concern, exploring the opportunities for fresh eyes to be cast over the areas in question by an internal critical friend can have significant impact very quickly. It will be for the organisation to determine how many such concerns will warrant this level of assurance, with the suggestion that this should be kept strictly to 'a few': in this definition it is suggested between one and three such concerns would be appropriate. If for example this was accepted by an organisation, then the identification of four areas of concern would warrant a RED no assurance level. An amber evaluation of partial assurance – with improvements required does recognise that considerable assurance has been made available regarding the optimum delivery or performance within a given portfolio of work, but again clearly recognises those few areas that are considered to present an *unacceptable risk* to the organisation and that require immediate executive and managerial action to be taken.

What Is the Significance of the Definition of 'Significant Assurance – with Minor Improvement Opportunities'?

The next level up is represented as GREEN and providing significant assurance – with minor improvement opportunities. This level of assurance can only be realised if the operational systems and controls to deliver the portfolio of work in question are in place and working effectively. There may be a few or many adjustments or improvements that have been recognised as *desirable* relating to a few or a wide range of issues. The critically important aspect is that none of these issues will be considered vital to the achievement of the organisation's strategic objectives. Obviously if these areas of identified improvement are not addressed the likelihood of organisational risk could increase, so there should be an explicit commitment to addressing these within a reasonable timescale; with this timescale being cognisant of management capacity and wider organisational priorities.

What Is the Significance of the Definition of 'Full Assurance'?

The final level up is BLUE and providing full assurance. Obviously, this level of assurance reflects the establishment of consistently effective systems, processes and controls for delivering a given portfolio of work. Although there remains at this level the potential for there to be some adjustments or improvements that *could* be made, the critical difference being that these will purely relate to aiming to achieve the best practice possible; a recognition of being outstanding or the aspiration to innovate. It is appropriate to acknowledge at this level that not all attempts at being innovative are successful. Failure is a very real feature of innovation and if failure to innovate is experienced this should not affect the organisation's evaluation of full assurance.

Supporting the Work of Assurance Sub-Committees:

Trust sub committees established to oversee complex portfolios of work deemed critical to achieving the strategic aims and objectives of the organisation, that consider information presented to offer assurance of progress, will find the use of four clearly defined levels of assurance reflects the standards practice by external auditors and provides a robust framework for focusing attention, prioritising discussion and appropriately escalating issues to the trust board. Four clearly defined levels of assurance provide the opportunity for achieving consistent evaluation of evidence presented, removing the need for personal judgements to be made and significantly mitigating against the potential for selective blindness potentially present within individuals or the committee as a whole, to influence the validity of the agreements reached on the level of assurance available. The next chapter expands upon this and other opportunities for maximising the effectiveness of an assurance sub-committee.

Chapter Summary

The widespread practice of replicating the use of a three-level RAG rating for both operational implementation and strategic assurance is inconsistent with how assurance is measured across the NHS where this is undertaken and provided by independent external parties. Strategic assurance is usually being sought to be generated on a macro basis, to evidence the delivery or implementation of a wide range of initiatives or standards for a complex portfolio of work. Recognised best practice for evaluating assurance supports the use of four levels of assurance with a specific mid-point at which performance is deemed to be unacceptable. The four RAGB recommended levels of overall macro assurance being – BLUE full assurance, GREEN significant assurance with minor improvement opportunities, AMBER partial assurance with improvements required and RED no assurance.

Trusts are recommended to adopt detailed definitions that explain each of the four assurance levels, to replicate the standards of practice available via external auditors to promote consistency of understanding, application and interpretation of strategic assurance levels. These definitions explicitly referring to the design and effective operation of the existing system (for improvement), the effectiveness of controls in place, the potential impact upon the achievement of the organisation's strategic objectives, the risks to the organisation's reputation or other strategic risks and finally the significance of any managerial action identified as required to be taken.

Trust sub committees that use a clearly defined framework of four distinct levels of assurance will benefit by this focusing attention, prioritising discussion and enabling appropriately escalation of issues to the trust board. Four clearly defined levels of assurance provide the opportunity for achieving consistent evaluation of evidence presented, removing the need for personal judgements to be made and significantly mitigating against the potential for selective blindness potentially present within individuals or the committee, to influence the validity of the agreements reached on the level of assurance available.

Chapter 11
Effective Committee Working

What Is a Board Sub-committee There to Do and How Does It Do This?

The fifth and final key element of a robust organisational assurance framework is for there to be effective sub-committee working. A detailed guide for trust boards detailing the principles of good governance, developed by the National leadership Council[9] lays out all the aspects of a robust governance framework, necessary to optimise a board's effectiveness. This includes the statutorily required establishment of committees to enable accountability through advising the board regarding the reliability of internal controls. The main purpose of sub-committees is to provide assurance to the trust board regarding the implementation of the agreed organisational strategies. The number of sub committees tends to vary slightly from trust to trust, with all trust boards having the required remuneration and audit sub-committees, in addition to a few additional sub-committees that should reflect the strategic priorities of the organisation. This may include as an example a sub-committee on partnership working or development of the workforce, where these issues are of significant strategic importance. The provision of high-quality clinical services is clearly central to the ambition and aim of every NHS trust and as such, the effectiveness of any sub-committees charged with overseeing this fundamental aspect of performance is vital to the achievement of this national ambition. This providing the rationale for the assessing of the effectiveness of both the trust board together with sub-committees of the trust board as being an important element of the overall organisational 'well – led review' undertaken for all NHS trusts by the CQC.

It is a requirement for all such committees for the chair to be a non-executive director, with the membership also including additional non-executive representation. With the role of NEDs being to both develop organisational strategy and review the performance of executive directors the opportunity these committees offer for scrutiny and objective review of executive performance to provide assurance of the implementation of strategic objectives is considerable. The practicalities of the predominately NED membership will necessitate individual NEDs chairing some committees, whilst being a member of others. This offered a powerful integrated arrangement of utilising NED expertise. However, the limitations of NED time as all appointments are made on a part time basis of usually less that one day per week, and the scope and complexity of the remits of sub committees present more than a few very practical challenges in doing justice to the volume and range of information that may potentially be presented to these committees. It is very easy for such committees to find an operational enthusiasm for demonstrating progress in certain areas to result in an overcrowded agenda containing long discursive reports of issues encountered and initiatives being progressed to address these issues. If this scenario is allowed to develop and establish itself as normal practice, the likelihood is that NEDs will find themselves taking longer and longer considering reports and seeking clarification on issues and less and less time on evaluating effectively the degree to which assurance has been provided of progress. In terms of NEDs determining what any outstanding priority executive management actions might be, that becomes akin to looking for a needle in a haystack.

What Prevents Sub-committees from Being Effective and How Can These Issues Be Addressed?

I have noticed that organisations often recognise that the committee arrangements are not working as they need or wish them to. This may present as frustration from NEDs in the volume and nature of reports they are being asked to consider, frustration from executives regarding the time required to prepare and contribute to these meetings or the chair's difficulty in determining the significance of what to bring to the attention of the trust board. Frustration can also be present from board members not directly engaged in the workings of specific committees who feel uninformed by the update reports provided to the board by the committee. The chair of the trust may equally be frustrated with the slow pace of achieving strategic objectives. This situation can often continue for considerable time with growing frustrations reflecting a widespread lack of understanding of what needs to be done to increase the focus of committee time and the strength of assurance generated on the progress being sought. At this point, an external party is often invited to undertake a 'governance review'. Engaging an independent external critical friend to review governance arrangements can be a very effective way to identify opportunities for adjusting systems and processes to provide assurance. If you feel you have a need to review local governance arrangements but there is a reduced appetite for engaging an external party to assist with this, take heart as there is much you will be able to consider doing internally and very easily to identify some of the potential barriers to effective committee working and make some easy adjustments to improve their effectiveness.

Acknowledging the benefits of and opportunities for developing internal independence, a senior colleague not directly involved in the workings of a given committee, could be identified to undertake a straightforward desk top review of some key documentation and undertake some direct observations of the committees working to provide some feedback and offer some potential adjustment options for considerations. Taking some time for a 'fresh eyes' review of the most fundamental of documentation pertaining to the committee's annual work plan, specific agendas, presented papers, recorded minutes and the assurance report to the trust board, will enable issues to be tracked from the strategic intent as reflected in an annual work plan, through to scheduled meetings, information to support discussions and recordings of findings and appropriate escalations. This level of review will not be required to extend across the entire remit of the committee's work but can be highly effective to be undertaken for a few specific issues, with a view to identifying weaknesses that if corrected will impact upon the entire remit and the effectiveness of the committee as a whole. Hopefully, each committee will have an annual work plan, and this plan comprehensively reflect every single aspect of the committee's remit. It is equally important that each individual committee work plan is cognisant of the annual plans of other committees, for example, two separate committees for quality and workforce, might each have an annual plan that reflects a given time to undertake the requirement to consider, refine and endorse annual priorities arising from their given agreed strategies. Given the interdependencies that will lie between quality and workforce strategies, it would be advantageous for the work of both committees to reflect this with the quality committee proactively seeking input from the workforce committee on the annual priorities for the quality strategy so that this input informs the discussions of the quality committee prior to endorsing these priorities. Similarly, the benefits of there being a scheduled opportunity for the quality committee to proactively provide the workforce committee with views prior to their consideration and endorsement of annual priorities for the workforce strategy would also be highly beneficial to be reflected in each committee's annual plan. An annual plan that is both comprehensive and reflects the interdependencies between committees creates a strong basis for effective working with clearly scheduled opportunities for all committee to consider all essential issues in a timely manner.

Once there is confidence in the framework provided by a comprehensive annual work plan, reviewing the committee's agendas to identify if they reflect both long term and emerging current priorities should be straightforward. A comprehensive work plan should enable regular consideration is given to longer term priorities. If consideration of these issues is being affected by an increasing number of unforeseen emerging priorities, clearer criteria for the threshold for presenting issues to the committee might be required or the timings and frequency of committee meeting may need to be altered to provide some much-needed additional capacity. Well-prepared committee meetings that have a consistent membership, a realistic agenda and that focus discussions between trust board meeting to allow for reflection, production of minutes and administration to provide meaningful reports to the trust board in a timely way are likely to have most impact upon influencing decisions taken by the board.

Observation of the committee in operation should identify if the integrated NED membership across committees is indeed providing the strong NED representation, challenge and leadership required by all committees. Is there evidence of collaboration across different assurance committees? Are there examples of NEDs promoting joint working with committees and informing the work of each other? Do discussions focus on seeking defined levels of assurance or alternatively are often stuck in seeking clarification and receiving reassurance? These are all aspects of behaviours that a regulator would look for when attending committee meetings to observe their working. A committee that receives reports of progress regarding the implementation of a complex improvement plan based on a simple three-level RAG approach is likely to have to seek lengthy clarification on the rationale for these three broad ranges. Conversely, a committee that receives reports of progress regarding the implementation of a complex improvement plan based on a significantly more detailed and defined seven-level evaluation approach which provides clear explicit rational for each evaluation, will be able to immediately focus on the issues of most concern and relevance, especially if this information may be presented by an independent manager not directly responsible for the delivery of the work plan in question. In this scenario, a committee using the four recommended levels of overall macro assurance to agree the level of assurance available regarding an entire portfolio of work such as the delivery of an improvement plan using the defined levels of full assurance, significant assurance with minor improvement opportunities, partial assurance with improvements required and no assurance, will be able to swiftly and consistently agree the level of assurance to be accepted and the issues to be escalated to the trust board.

Another area of review that can be extremely enlightening to undertake is to assess the degree to which the recorded minutes of the meeting have accurately reflected the discussions that took place, including explicit management actions required to be taken to address the limitations of assurance received to date. If for example, minutes accurately reflect the imitations of contributions from some members, then an easy step would be to explore with these individuals the reasons for this so that a better balance of contributions may be achieved. If minutes aren't accurately reflecting the nature of discussions taking place, which is a very common occurrence, this must swiftly be addressed so that all members of the board who should have access to all sub-committee minutes are able to appreciate the accurate and representative detail of the committees working. Without this, it will be very difficult for board members not directly involved in the work of specific committees to proactively contribute to the working of that committee. Only when the perspectives and contributions of all board members are sought and made available to all committees will they be able to optimise their potential and begin to work as intended and required.

In addition to the production and circulation of minutes, it is common practice for each committee to provide a highlight report to the board. All too often one can find such reports as following an internally derived template which simply seeks to summarise what issues were considered as part of the agenda and outlying what the intentions of the committee are going forward. Such reports are often given little agenda time as the primary response they can generate is 'so what?'. Given that the purpose of these committees is to seek, provide and confirm the assurance of delivery of agreed portfolios of work that are of significant strategic importance, the most impactful reports are those that clearly identify the level of assurance provided for each portfolio of work. Within this, providing explicit clarity of the identification of any organisational risks, and the extent of any managerial action to be taken as a matter of priority. As part of such a report, explicit requests for actions to be taken by or support sought from any other sub committees would indicate highly effective integrated working. Similarly reports that state clearly any recommendations regarding aspects of strategic development deemed as required, or the need for resources of any nature to support committee working or strategic implementation, evidence a highly effective evidence-based approach to influencing decision making undertaken by the board.

Chapter Summary

Often an organisation can recognise that the committee arrangements are not working as they wish or need them to, and this can continue for considerable time due to a lack of understanding of what needs to be done to increase the focus of committee time and the strength of assurance generated. There is much that a trust can do very easily to identify some of the potential barriers to effective committee working and make some easy adjustments to improve their effectiveness. Some key questions to ask being:

- Is there an annual work plan and an agenda that balances long term and emerging priorities?
- Is there strong cross committee NED representation, challenge and leadership?
- Do discussions focus on seeking levels of assurance using four detailed defined levels?
- Is there evidence of collaborative cross committee working?
- Are minutes accurate and reflective of discussions? Are they available to all board members to promote proactive contribution?
- Do committees explicitly influence the work of other committees and trust board decision making?

If these questions are not able to be positively answered in full, simple steps to strengthen these areas of performance will significantly help in developing a committee's focus towards consistently defining the level of assurance received. With the role of NEDs being to both develop organisational strategy and review the performance of executive directors the opportunity that NED led effective committee working offers for undertaking scrutiny and objective review of executive performance to provide assurance of the implementation of strategic objectives is considerable.

Chapter 12
Eradicating Selective Blindness Across the NHS

The political landscape regarding priorities for NHS improvement is currently relatively unclear and feels relatively unstable. This in part due within a relatively short period of time, to the multiple changes of key NHS leaders at the Department of Health, who have a remit to provide strategic leadership regarding NHS improvement priorities. It would probably also likely to be considered fair to state that widespread confidence within the NHS is extremely low regarding the potential for this situation changing significantly very soon. A Health Secretary for a brief period of time, Theresa Coffey sought to reassure us that she had a grip on the strategic priorities by taking a leaf from the book of Jeremy Vine broadcasting where for those who are unfamiliar with his Radio two lunchtime show, he seeks to introduce his show to the listeners in four words to summarise the nature of discussions to take place in the following hours. This approach is generally well received by the multitasking listeners of his daytime current affairs programme. One can only presume that the government's summary of NHS urgent and important priorities using the mnemonic ABCD, seeks to convey to clinicians, the general public and patients that they understand the complexities of the difficulties being experienced, with an easy to recall path set to overcome these focusing on the represented areas of ambulance handovers, backlog waiting, care and doctors and dentists. The A within this mnemonic, represents an ever-escalating national concerns regarding extended ambulance turnaround times. The documentation of the most rudimentary of RCA would serve to provide multiple examples of evidence that most problems with accessing the front door of a hospital are directly linked to the limited ability to open the back door to facilitate an exit: this process significantly reduced by the ever-increasing number of patients in acute beds awaiting transfer to an intermediate care or social care facility. The relentless existing focus being exerted on trusts by external stakeholders to direct efforts towards addressing recognised contributing factors that affect bed utilisation and an effective flow of patients through a hospital setting rather than the evidenced root cause, must stop. Whilst all parties are seeking for patients to receive the right care at the right time from the right professionals in the right setting, and there may undoubtedly be contributing local contributing causes related to staffing, equipment, facilities, operational procedures, defined pathways of care for given conditions, that may potentially marginally improve ambulance turnaround times, focusing attention towards these issues in the absence of a commitment to addressing the identified root cause – the solutions for which lies wholly external to the NHS, will at best only deliver some discrete, marginal and absolutely unsustainable improvements. We have got to do better than this. The NHS needs our politicians to do better than this.

With NHS statistics showing that at the height of the summer 2022, 13,338 patients who had no recorded medical need were residing in a hospital bed, NHS acute services are grinding to a halt. Despite the lack of home care and places in rehabilitation or care homes being identified as the reason for these increasing delays, trusts continue to receive instructions to implement new national initiatives to increase patient flow; the latest of these being to implement the additional 'boarding' of medically fit patients in acute wards. These patients being over and above the bed or staffing capacity of the wards but considered nationally to be an acceptable approach to mitigating the acute risks associated with having no beds to admit acutely ill patients. For those of you who have worked in the NHS for as long as I have, you might recall that this practice of having an 'extra' patient boarding on an acute ward awaiting discharge was accepted some decades past as common practice and, indeed viewed as being in the patients best interest. The critical difference of the circumstances in place at this time being that wards were strongly specialty orientated so the patient being 'boarded' would be known by the ward nurses, wards routinely had patient sitting/dining rooms which provided an appropriate environment for the patient to wait prior to discharge, wards optimally operated at less than full capacity if anything failed to go to plan, and the patient's discharge arrangements were always in place with the likelihood being that the patient was simply waiting for a family member to collect them. The current circumstances whereby trusts are being required to 'board' additional medically fit patients across all acute wards could not be more different. The risks associated with this latest national initiative being considerable relating directly to the increased acuity of acutely ill patients, nursing vacancy factors necessitating high use of temporary staff, the routine bed capacity operating model presenting no ability to respond to the unexpected, and the absence of confirmed domestic/community care packages. With the heart of this book being the importance of truly identifying the root cause of a problem to have any confidence in implementing a sustainable solution to that problem, you will recognise this latest initiative as pointless as it simply seeks – with more than a hint of desperation, to give the impression of having a solution, whilst focusing on addressing a contributory factor of not having enough beds rather than the root cause of the increasing numbers of medically fit patients residing in acute beds, being the absence of social care packages of care. If the government wants to use a mnemonic to demonstrate understanding of current issues, a simpler ABC to represent Assessments for discharge, Blocked beds and Care packages might have conveyed a better understanding of the systemic issues requiring to be addressed as a solution to existing challenges!

This level of uncertainty and lack of confidence in the situation improving, hugely affects both the focus and momentum of local trust improvements. The timing of this book is intended to support healthcare professionals through this protracted period of uncertainty to harness the available expertise and commitment to improve services. This recognising the extent to which the vast majority of those who work within the NHS, despite huge frustrations with aspects of it, love and value it. Wishing to see it thrive and realise its potential for future generations. One of the aspirations of book is based, is that the challenging context within which all NHS trusts continue to operate may be recognised by readers as presenting an opportunity to gain some control of determining their improvement priorities by using this book as a self-help guide. Its contents are quickly digestible. To those of you perhaps concerned that limitations of experience or specialist knowledge maybe affecting your personal effectiveness, I have tried to truthfully and positively distil and translate my learning from working with multiple trusts from all healthcare sectors that have with differing levels of success all notably attempted to improve services. Whether you are primarily positioned at the bedside or in the boardroom, consider the clear principles upon which existing trust arrangements can be easily reviewed at any level within an organisation, without the necessity for external involvement or potentially uncomfortable exposure for individuals or leadership teams. Additional resources are not required for progress to be made. An appetite to continually improve and open mind will. I have attempted to optimise the practical opportunities for all trusts to potential increase their potential to improve and offer individuals simple achievable options for strengthening their existing ways of working and assuring the delivery of progress. Take from the contents what you feel able to try, start wherever seems most appropriate for your circumstances and be pragmatic regarding application. I have deliberately not sought to name and shame but anonymised and generalised to provide examples and explanations to stimulate thinking. I hope you will feel that this is the case and whilst you have been digesting the pages have been able to identify some achievable, straightforward steps you might have an appetite for exploring further?

With the CQC's State of care report published in October 2021[10] evidencing that NHS staff are exhausted and the workforce depleted, we need now more than ever to increase our ability to influence beyond the boardroom and specifically members of His Majesties Government (HMG) or those senior colleagues working on his behalf, to ensure the precious national treasure that is our NHS continues to develop and improve, to be available to support the next generation from cradle to grave as it has for the post World War 2 generation and their descendants. This can seem to be a herculean 'ask' given the endemic degree of political selective blindness that seems to be increasing and impacting all ability of the NHS to improve. Most spectacularly evidenced by the ongoing failure to acknowledge the lack of a long-term financial settlement for social care being the root cause of the NHS continuing to grind to a halt. There is no other alternative than we must overcome all aspects of selective blindness at both and individual and organisational level if the NHS is to have any chance of surviving and thriving as those that love and value it as institutions wishes it to do. To achieve this all NHS trusts need to fully optimise their local internal arrangements for improving services within their individual organisations PRIOR to having any reasonable expectation that they might be able to increase their sphere of influence to external stakeholders such as commissioners, regulators or members of HMG. I believe that EVERY trust no matter how well performing it is, has the potential of strengthening its existing approach to improving services even further. More importantly such high performing organisations should be identifying how they can share their learning to support other organisations possibly viewed as currently struggling. It will only be when a sizable critical mass of trusts can demonstrate and evidence that they have overcome local aspects of selective blindness that we will find we have the leverage to expose, call out and seek to overcome the selective blindness evident in those in lofty positions with legitimate power and authority to influence the future of the NHS.

At the beginning of this book, we explored how one can begin to identify the extent to which a trust has the potential to improve. This by examining if it can demonstrate if it has:

- a firm grip of both urgent and important issues,
- the necessary pace and momentum of work to address issues,
- evidence of sustained improvement over time.

We recognised the value of considering a simple desk top review of relevant documents to identify if there was evidence of an absolute focus on both urgent and important priorities, the necessary effective staff engagement and understanding of improvement priorities, an explicit recognition and a commitment to addressing the systemic causes of variation and a clear and compelling strategic narrative that describes a path to success. This very simple action of undertaking a structured document review being able to be undertaken quickly and easily to take stoke of the organisation's available evidence of potential to improve. The findings offering the opportunity to strengthen the documentation if considered it fails to do justice to existing working or providing a focus of attention for internal development. These important aspects of self-assessment acting as a precursor to the introduction of the five key characteristic elements identified as required to be present within an organisation's effective assurance framework, which we have explored in detail. Although all elements of an effective assurance framework are of equal importance, and trusts can choose to begin to strengthen any aspect or several aspects simultaneously, the fundamental basis upon which sustainable improvement may be realised is without doubt, that the true root-cause of an issue of concern is correctly identified and any agreed initiatives clearly directed towards addressing this root cause rather than the symptom of this cause. The importance of analysing the root cause as a collaborative utilising differing experience, perspectives, knowledge and available data and the necessity to document this to begin to overcome selective blindness evident across the organisation or health system cannot be overstated. This approach alone will begin to develop the necessary recognition of systemic root causes of variation, previously considered too difficult to identify or address. As increasing numbers of trusts generate more documented evidence of the true root causes of performance concerns, and local irrefutable documentary evidence mounts of the real national barriers to NHS performance and the improvement of services, the ability of commissioners, regulators and HMG to ignore the significance of these issues will begin to erode. Such an approach also serves to protect senior trust directors and clinicians who may have been fearful to date, to voice too loudly what the root causes are. We have many courageous experienced individuals in leadership positions in trusts who the NHS cannot afford to lose, who know only too well where the root causes of NHS poor performance lie. We can support these individuals by ensuring all local root causes of variation for every trust are identified, recognised, documented and shared. Rather than risk being viewed as a troublemaker, the generation of evidence of the primary root cause/s resulting in a wide variety of symptomatic concerns as presented within a SMART 'plus' improvement plan, will significantly mitigate this risk through the cascade of documented evidence confirming root cause/s requiring to be addressed. The widespread production of SMART 'plus' Improvement plans that document root causes of variation will further provide some protection for individuals by reinforcing that whilst it will be right and proper to hold senior individuals within the NHS to account for addressing the root causes that are within the influence of the NHS provider organisations to address, it would be wholly inappropriate to seek to do so for root causes beyond the parameters of the trust/NHS. Such plans will reinforce the futility of any attempt made to hold senior individuals within the NHS to account for delivering improvements evidenced as relating directly to root causes NOT within the ability of the NHS to address. As an optimist, I am hopeful that if trusts improve the extent to which they routinely undertake RCA to identify the systemic root causes of their local symptomatic concerns, this will contribute to reducing the emotion and frustration that presently surround widespread national performance concerns where the root cause of concerns does not lie within the influence of any part of the NHS to influence directly.

We have explored in detail how we can improve the local approaches being taken, by ensuring SMART 'plus' improvement plans document all fundamental root causes of variation and commit to initiatives directed to addressing these in addition to utilising a seven-stepped approach to evaluating progress to strengthen consistency of evaluation and reporting of overall progress. Taking explicit action to strengthen the degree of internal independence present at various stages of the improvement cycle has also been identified as not requiring expert knowledge or a huge time commitment, but fresh eyes and a consistent approach to reviewing all aspect of the improvement cycle and feeding back these observations as a critical friend can significantly reduce duplication, errors and inaccuracies to contribute to a clearer assessment being made of the impact of actions taken to date and the subsequent formal reporting. It is reasonable to view the strengthening of internal independence to mitigate the risk of familiarisation and self-review to be possible for all trusts regardless of the level of confidence held in existing arrangements, and for the wider benefits from this approach to be seen in terms of improved use of assurance sub-committee time an improvement of the level of grip, momentum of progress and the sustainability of improvements being achieved across the organisation.

Hopefully, I have done enough to generate an appetite within you to consider moving away from a RAG rating system towards a more effective seven-level operational evaluation rating? The optimum words here being 'move towards'. If you find recognition of the limitations of a three-level RAG evaluation but scepticism regarding the benefits of the granularity of seven levels, then have confidence to take steps to move *away* from three levels and *towards* seven levels. Utilising an explicitly detailed approach that requires an evaluation to be made upon the three aspects of delivery of agreed initiatives/actions, the identification and addressing of underlying causes and the measurement of outcomes, presents a highly effective basis for an explicit understanding of progress to be swiftly and widely agreed upon with minimum application of professional judgements potentially influenced by aspects of selective blindness, the reasons for which may be experiential or knowledge based. The critical focus on evaluating outcomes also serves to highlight the importance and validity of the RCA undertaken and the need for these aspects to be revisited where outcomes are not being achieved as desired. The significance of the delivery of desired outcomes was represented by the single GREEN level within this framework indicating the achievement of these. The final and optimal level representing sustainable improvement of these outcomes over an extended period and the ultimate formal transfer of ongoing performance management to business as usual.

I hope I have also done enough to encourage you to recognise what is available to us to learn from best practice from top global accountancy firms specialising in audit and assurance such as Deloitte LLP, PwC and KPMG, and the application of best practice for defining levels of strategic judgement as reflected by the CQC and Ofsted. I hope I have stimulated an appetite within you to actively explore the benefits in embracing four levels of assurance, each with detailed definitions to standardise application. I have presented a clear case for the use of detailed definitions for BLUE full assurance, GREEN significant assurance with minor improvement opportunities, AMBER partial assurance with improvements required and RED no assurance. Each explicitly referring to the design and effective operation of the existing system (for improvement), the effectiveness of controls in place, the potential impact upon the achievement of the organisation's strategic objectives and finally, the risks to the organisation's reputation or other strategic risks and the significance of any managerial action identified as required to be taken. We have explored how trust sub-committees that use a clearly defined framework of four distinct levels of assurance will benefit by this focusing and prioritising discussion in addition to supporting the appropriate escalation of issues to the trust board. Trust sub-committees established to oversee complex portfolios of work deemed critical to achieving the strategic aims and objectives of the organisation, that consider information presented to offer assurance of progress, will find the use of four clearly defined levels of assurance reflects the standards practice by external auditors and serve to provide the opportunity for achieving consistent evaluation of evidence presented, reducing the need for personal judgements to be made and significantly mitigating against the potential for selective blindness potentially present within individuals or indeed at this level present within any committee. This significantly influencing both the validity of the agreements and the confidence held in these agreements reached on the level of assurance available. Given that we have recognised the purpose of these committees being to seek, provide and confirm the assurance of delivery of agreed portfolios of work that are of significant strategic importance, it is obvious that the most impactful reports from these committees are those that clearly identify the level of assurance provided for each complex portfolio of work. Such reports providing explicit clarity of the identification of any organisational risks and the extent of any managerial action to be taken as a matter of priority. Organisational risk as we've discussed being measured in terms of the strategic objectives and priorities of the organisation and the identified risks to achieving these. This brings us full circle to the remaining question to be posed to assess the organisations potential to improve: that question being, is there a clear strategic narrative that describes a path to success? It is essential that the specific organisation's strategic narrative must be used consistently as the metrics against which the significance of any undesirable variations identified and any risk to addressing variation is assessed and evaluated in term of the impact this risk presents to the delivery of strategic objectives.

A SMART 'plus' improvement plan; a healthy degree of internal challenge created using independent critical friends to provide feedback on key stages of the improvement cycle; an explicit move away from a simple RAG rating of operational progress towards a more detailed seven-stepped approach based upon evaluations of root causes, initiatives and outcomes, as well as applying best practice strategic assurance definitions and levels offering significant yet simple, easy and effective opportunities for every trust to further strengthen its ability to improve services sustainably. Evidencing such an approach, grounded in best practice and underpinned with evidence that has been independently challenged and refined, presents a solid foundation for continuing the discussions with external stakeholders to engage, inform, educate and begin to challenge their perception of what is required to improve performance across the NHS.

So, with the looming cloud of collective defeatism casting an increasing shadow across our NHS family, the key question for you as the reader, is do you have the appetite and energy to consider applying some of the principles, processes and practices detailed within the preceding chapters and summarised above? I hope so because there will be something that could help everyone in these pages and currently all manner of help is needed. The potential of each trust making progress with this approach in some small way is not only in the increased level of control and influence that can be generated to motivate individuals to continue seeking to improve services, but also in the establishment of a supportive understanding that can be generated across organisations. Working collectively to build a momentum towards exposing individual and collective selective blindness wherever this is present and where this so damaging in continuing to hold back the NHS from delivering high quality services will also have a positive effect of dispersing the cloud of effective defeatism which is currently affecting us all.

Just prior to finalising these pages the CQC published its state of care report for 2021–2022[11]. For those of us close to the NHS, there were no surprises in this report, but if one views these annual reports as a potential outline improvement plan for the NHS, then one should acknowledge that in the contents of this year's report, CQC would appear to have done as much as it is able to clearly evidence and articulate what it considers to be the root cause of why more people are currently dissatisfied with the NHS than satisfied. This compelling report outlines all the symptomatic failings as a consequence of the confirmed root cause identified as being a lack of social care grid locking the whole health system. With the CQC having done what is within its gift to do, I'm hoping that for that which we love and value such as the NHS and the NHS family of which we are proud to be a member, that we will have retained some optimism and belief that each of us can still make a difference, that we do all have the ability to increase our sphere of influence and that in acting together, we can continue to build an evidenced based momentum towards exposing individual and collective selective blindness beyond the boardroom, where this has without doubt been shown over recent years to be the single biggest risk to the future of the NHS.

---

[1] Hooper G, 'Trust Building Measures', Director, 2004

[2] Review of CQC's impact on quality and improvement in health and social care. April 2017

[3] www.cqc.org.uk/guidance-providers/healthcare/key-lines-enquiry-healthcare-services

[4] www.england.nhs.uk/recoverysupport

[5] www.cqc.org.uk/drivingimprovement

[6] www.gov.uk/assuranceframeworksguidance

[7] www.nhsproviders.org/media/1182/board-assurance-a-tool-kit

[8] Hooper G, 'The NHS has suffered a critical loss of authentic internal challenge', HSJ, 2019

[9] The healthy NHS Board, Principles for Good Governance, National leadership Council

[10] The state of health care and adult social care in England 2020/21, CQC

[11] The state of health care and adult social care in England 2021/22, CQC